Healthy and Sustainable Fundraising Activities

Mobilizing Your Community Toward Social Responsibility

Jenine M. De Marzo, EdD

Adelphi University

Anne Gibbone, EdD

Adelphi University

Greg Letter, PhD

Adelphi University

Catherine I. Klein, PhD

Northcentral University

Human Kinetics

Library of Congress Cataloging-in-Publication Data

Healthy and sustainable fundraising activities : mobilizing your community toward social responsibility / Jenine M. De Marzo ... [et al.].
   p. cm.
 Includes bibliographical references.
 ISBN 978-1-4504-1281-0 (soft cover) -- ISBN 1-4504-1281-5 (soft cover)
 1. Educational fund raising--United States. 2. Community and school--United States. 3. Children--Health and hygiene--United States. I. De Marzo, Jenine M., 1964-
 LC241.H43 2012
 379.1'3--dc23
                        2012002865

ISBN-10: 1-4504-1281-5 (print)
ISBN-13: 978-1-4504-1281-0 (print)

The web addresses cited in this text were current as of January 27, 2012, unless otherwise noted.

Acquisitions Editor: Cheri Scott; **Developmental Editor:** Melissa Feld; **Assistant Editor:** Rachel Brito; **Copyeditor:** Patsy Fortney; **Permissions Manager:** Martha Gullo; **Graphic Designer:** Joe Buck; **Graphic Artist:** Denise Lowry; **Cover Designer:** Bob Reuther; **Art Manager:** Kelly Hendren; **Associate Art Manager:** Alan L. Wilborn; **Illustrations:** © Human Kinetics; **Printer:** Versa Press

Printed in the United States of America   10   9   8   7   6   5   4   3   2   1

The paper in this book is certified under a sustainable forestry program.

Human Kinetics
Website: www.HumanKinetics.com

United States: Human Kinetics, P.O. Box 5076, Champaign, IL 61825-5076
800-747-4457
e-mail: humank@hkusa.com

Canada: Human Kinetics, 475 Devonshire Road Unit 100, Windsor, ON N8Y 2L5
800-465-7301 (in Canada only)
e-mail: info@hkcanada.com

Europe: Human Kinetics, 107 Bradford Road, Stanningley, Leeds LS28 6AT, United Kingdom
+44 (0) 113 255 5665
e-mail: hk@hkeurope.com

Australia: Human Kinetics, 57A Price Avenue, Lower Mitcham, South Australia 5062
08 8372 0999
e-mail: info@hkaustralia.com

New Zealand: Human Kinetics, P.O. Box 80, Torrens Park, South Australia 5062
0800 222 062
e-mail: info@hknewzealand.com

E5502

Contents

1 Fundraising 101

2 Extending Your Fundraising Potential

3 Low-Level Fundraisers

4 Midlevel Fundraisers

5 High-Level Fundraisers

Preface

Historically, schools and community organizations in the United States have relied on fundraisers to bridge budget gaps and help pay for basic supplies, field trips, athletic and musical equipment, and after-school activities. Despite the rising rates of childhood obesity in recent years, those fundraisers all too often rely on the sale of calorie-dense, low-nutrient junk food or low-quality or unnecessary products.

Currently, the need for fundraisers is increasing because U.S. public schools are falling under severe financial stress as states slash education spending and drain federal stimulus money that has until recently staved off deep classroom cuts and widespread job losses. School districts have already suffered big budget cuts since the economic recession began in 2008, but experts say the cash crunch will get a lot worse as states run out of stimulus dollars. Community groups are also having difficulty sustaining their programming efforts. Fewer and fewer families have the luxury of sending their children to after-school pay-for-play activities.

California's financial crisis continues to put the squeeze on already strapped public schools as state lawmakers work to close a $20 billion deficit. The effects of this situation will be staggering in the years to come. New York, a state that serves a disproportionate number of students in need, stands to take hits in school aid, local government assistance, social services, and transportation under the current and proposed state budget.

Communities throughout the United States and across the globe face similar situations: more teacher layoffs, larger class sizes, smaller paychecks, fewer classroom electives, and disappearing extracurricular activities. After-school programs and community agencies are often the hardest hit as budgets disappear. Perhaps schools and community organizations can use this unfortunate crisis to target resources in a way that better serves their constituents.

Healthy and Sustainable Fundraising Activities provides fundraising ideas to complement the nutrition, physical activity, and health messages taught in the classroom while remaining eco-friendly. Schools and community agencies *can* raise money in a way that doesn't compromise student and community health or the ecosystem. In response to the deterioration of the health of many young people, Feingold (1999, p. 2) wrote: "We as adult leaders can take charge and reform the way we educate and interact with youth." To this end, we need to sustain a broad multidisciplinary and integrative perspective that emphasizes our children's health, physical activity, and wellness while never losing sight of our responsibility to help them grow from children to adolescents to socially competent adult citizens (Feingold, 1999).

Fundraising activities can enhance community wellness by fostering positive attitude development, values education, cooperative social experiences, cultural sensitivity, and a general appreciation and respect for the greater society. All of these things can be accomplished while developing a high regard for wellness and an increased sensitivity to the value of hard work, perseverance, honesty, civic engagement, integrity, and self-reflection.

For the first time in U.S. history, many of the highest government officials have acknowledged that American youth are facing a health crisis that is likely to affect the nation's physical and fiscal health for years to come. As a result of this growing public awareness, U.S. lawmakers passed the Child Nutrition and Women, Infants and Children (WIC) Reauthorization Act of 2004 (Sec. 204 of P.L. 108-205), also known as the Federal Wellness Policy. Issued in June of 2006, this law helped launch a national effort to combat childhood obesity.

Using a community-based health promotion approach, *Healthy and Sustainable Fundraising Activities* involves the whole community (families, educators, voluntary and community-based organizations, faith communities, local health care institutions and providers, government organizations, and the media) in health-promoting activities. By approaching fundraising in this holistic and comprehensive way, we can positively affect long-term health behaviors. Change may begin at the individual or family level, but maintaining change relies on reinforcement and approval at the community level. Programs that focus on the whole community have a positive effect on factors that place people at risk. The activities in this book serve these purposes.

Studies show that most people want to lead healthy lives and are eager to improve their lifestyles. In fact, many people attempt to change unhealthy behaviors, only to fail. Most health promotion strategies assist individuals, yet by affecting whole communities it is possible to influence long-lasting successful behavior change. *Healthy and Sustainable Fundraising Activities* make it possible for the community to support healthy behaviors while financially supporting schools and other organizations.

The United States is facing unprecedented pressure to educate young people so they can compete in the global market. Technology and dynamic financial changes are constantly redefining the essential skills necessary for young people to succeed in the 21st century. Activities in this book reflect the student outcomes outlined by the Partnership for 21st Century Skills (www.p21.org). These outcomes focus on the specific skills, content knowledge, expertise, and literacy students need to succeed in a changing work environment. These outcomes address life and career skills; learning and innovation skills; and information, media, and technology skills. Students also need to study core academic subjects and 21st century themes.

Because every community is unique, it is not our intent to suggest that there is only one way to implement a program. In fact, you should feel free to take the material here and adapt it to fit your own community and organization. Some of the material will be applicable to your project, whereas other material will not. Choose what works best for your group. Most materials can be revised for any health promotion activity.

Schools, clubs, parent–teacher organizations, and athletic departments may be reluctant to stop using the fundraisers they have used for years. To meet such challenges, *Healthy and Sustainable Fundraising Activities* provides fundraising ideas, flyer templates, sample press releases, and other documents to make new events profitable and enjoyable. In 2007, the nonprofit Center for Science in the Public Interest (CSPI) released the report "Sweet Deals: School Fundraising Can Be Healthy and Profitable" showing that nonfood and healthy food fundraising options can raise as much or more than the traditional junk food fundraisers. Margo G. Wootan of CPSI said, "It is time to junk the junk food fundraisers. As a society we are sure to spend more on the resulting diet-related diseases than we could ever hope to raise selling junk food in schools."

This book provides a wide range of nonfood, eco-friendly, and physically active fundraising options to choose from. Experience shows that these options can raise as much or more money than traditional junk food and product sales can while also increasing community health. Included are activities for all age groups that range from offering individual to large group participation.

Activity lesson plans help teachers, parents, coaches, or administrators create successful fundraising events. They follow a standard classroom lesson plan format that includes the following: educational objectives, targeted dimensions of health, standards met, age level, materials, recommended procedures, event preparation time line, postevent processing and evaluation, sustainable extension, and forms and templates.

Chapter 1 is all about fundraising basics to familiarize you with the general fundraising process including goal setting, setting up a plan of action, identifying your organization's primary and secondary targets, developing a preliminary budget, setting time lines, and coordinating multiple events. Chapter 2 explains the advantages of and how to use social networking sites in fundraising activities to make use of instant communication and information dissemination. The use of this technology will increase not only your success but also volunteers' technological literacy. This chapter also shows how to generate funds through donation networking and grant writing. We show you how to develop your own social networking page and how to use it before, during, and after your fundraising event.

Chapters 3 through 5 contain fundraising ideas, forms, and templates that you can use as is or adjust to your liking. The activities in chapter 3 are the simplest; most can be conducted by organization staff and inexperienced volunteers. Additionally, these activities require little maintenance over time and are often over and done within one day.

Chapter 4 contains activities that require a higher level of knowledge, skills, and abilities. Some involve an increased level of technological know-how, and others require increased youth supervision. Volunteers for these fundraisers may have to seek assistance outside of the immediate group.

The activities in chapter 5 require a high level of knowledge, skills, and abilities. An organizer with some experience or strong leadership skills is essential.

These activities can yield large profits, are geared toward corporations and social or community commerce (larger organizations or community businesses), and can take place in high-profile locations. Often, one well-crafted high-level fundraiser can take the place of several small ones throughout the year.

You may want to start with an activity from chapter 3 and move to more advanced activities as you gain confidence and success. Another option is to run several fundraisers concurrently or consecutively over the course of a year. Anyway you choose to use this book, all of the essential elements are in place to make your event a success.

One way that *Healthy and Sustainable Fundraising Activities* is unique is that we never lose sight of the big picture, which is promoting health and wellness within communities and among all participants. Each activity addresses some or all of three sets of U.S. national standards. The National Health Education standards represent the world-class ideal of developing the highest level of health education knowledge and skills so that youth may be healthy and achieve their academic potential. The National Association for Sport and Physical Education standards promote the development of physically educated people who will enjoy a lifetime of physical activity. The activities also reflect the outcomes advocated by the Partnership for 21st Century Skills: to provide young people with the skills, knowledge, and literacy to be successful in the 21st century. All of these standards are nestled under the umbrella of the six basic dimensions of health: physical, social, mental, emotional, spiritual, and environmental.

The activity finder identifies the standards and dimensions of health that each activity addresses. This will help you choose fundraising activities that are in line with the unique objectives and mission of your organization.

In addition to school professionals, coaches, athletic directors, and after-school coordinators, any organization that serves young people will find this book indispensable. This book can also be used as a supplemental guide by anyone interested in integrating the dimensions of health, wellness, and movement, as well as 21st century skills, into their programs. The majority of the activities use similar or limited resources often easily available to school, camp, and community-based groups.

Because each organization has unique skill sets, objectives, and missions, the activities in *Healthy and Sustainable Fundraising Activities* can be used as they appear or tweaked in various directions to suit the needs and desires of your group. Do not feel compelled to use these activities strictly as they appear; feel free to experiment and make them your own. The only true failure is in not trying at all. Each fundraising attempt provides a wealth of knowledge that can be applied to the next one.

How to Use the Activity Finder

Please take a few minutes to read this section so that you can use your copy of *Healthy and Sustainable Fundraising Activities* to motivate your students and volunteers, sustain your organization, and maximize your efforts.

The activities in this book are divided into three levels that are identified with lightbulb icons. One lightbulb indicates that the activity requires a low level of knowledge, skills, and abilities (chapter 3); two lightbulbs indicate more advanced activities (chapter 4); and three lightbulbs indicate activities that are the most challenging and demanding (chapter 5). The activities in chapters 4 and 5 are more challenging to organize and execute; however, they yield higher profits and often negate the necessity for multiple fundraising activities throughout the year.

Chapter 3 includes fundraising activities that require a low level of knowledge, skills, and abilities to be successful (one lightbulb). Most adults with little or no experience with fundraising can execute these activities. Student volunteers can be used in almost every one of the activities in chapter 3, and the materials required can be found in the average home or office. Any equipment needed can be borrowed from local community organizations in your neighborhood. Chapter 3 activities often yield low to moderate profits, but are easy to get off the ground. Many organizations employ two or more activities such as these over the course of a year or even have several occurring at once. Most of the activities in chapter 3 can be organized by one or two committed adults or a small committee.

Chapters 4 and 5 include activities and events that are more involved and require higher levels of skill in terms of knowledge, skills, and abilities. However after your organization has executed an activity or two from chapter 3, the skill set will be in place to tackle more advanced events. Many organizations stack events, which means they run events concurrently. For example, an organization may hold the Seniors for Seniors: An Evening of Dance event, and hold a silent auction at the very same event for maximum fundraising. We have found that the advanced skills are easily attained or are found within your organization's volunteer pool.

Every activity in this book lists the educational standards it addresses, thereby helping organizations elucidate their mission of educating and guiding young people. Also listed for each activity are the dimensions of health the activity addresses. The six dimensions of health are physical, social, mental, emotional, spiritual, and environmental.

Each activity also lists the Framework for 21st Century Learning (www. p21.org) outcomes that it promotes to support our young people in an ever-changing world. The student outcomes are life and career skills; learning and innovation skills; and information, media, and technology skills.

National Health Education standards (The Joint Commission on National Health Education Standards, American Cancer Society, 2007) are also listed for every activity. These eight standards generally address students' ability to comprehend, analyze, communicate, utilize, and demonstrate health concepts and skills.

National Association for Sport and Physical Education (NASPE) standards for physical education are also listed for many of the fundraising activities in this book (www.aahperd.org/naspe/standards/nationalStandards). These standards are provided to help you align the activity with your physical activity objectives by integrating physical activities in varied and meaningful ways.

Healthy and Sustainable Fundraising Activities will help you make an educated choice about fundraising that is based on your organization's mission, beliefs, financial need, and fundraising acumen. Generally, we recommend starting with an activity in chapter 3; as your skill set and confidence increase, you can choose more difficult or more demanding fundraisers from chapters 4 and 5. Keep in mind that you can use the activities in this book as they appear or as templates from which to create your own activities to suit your particular needs.

Activity Finder

TARGETED DIMENSIONS OF HEALTH

Physical

Social

Mental

Emotional

Spiritual

Environmental

21ST CENTURY STUDENT OUTCOMES

Life and Career Skills

Today's world requires far more thinking skills and content knowledge and the ability to navigate the complexities of life and work as well as global communities.

Learning and Innovation Skills

Students must be prepared to think creatively and critically and be adept at communication and collaboration.

Information, Media, and Technology Skills

As our environment becomes more media and technology infused, 21st century learners must have the functional knowledge and skills necessary for successfully contributing to society.

LEVEL OF SKILL REQUIRED

Low

Moderate

High

NATIONAL HEALTH EDUCATION STANDARDS

Standard 1: Students will comprehend concepts related to health promotion and disease prevention to enhance health.

Standard 2: Students will analyze the influence of family, peers, culture, media, technology, and other factors on health behaviors.

Standard 3: Students will demonstrate the ability to access valid information, products, and services to enhance health.

Standard 4: Students will demonstrate the ability to use interpersonal communication skills to enhance health and avoid or reduce health risks.

Standard 5: Students will demonstrate the ability to use decision-making skills to enhance health.

Standard 6: Students will demonstrate the ability to use goal-setting skills to enhance health.

Standard 7: Students will demonstrate the ability to practice health-enhancing behaviors and avoid or reduce health risks.

Standard 8: Students will demonstrate the ability to advocate for personal, family, and community health.

Reprinted from Joint Committee on National Health Education Standards, 2007, *National health education standards: Achieving excellence*, 2nd ed. (Atlanta: American Cancer Society).

NATIONAL ASSOCIATION FOR SPORT AND PHYSICAL EDUCATION (NASPE) NATIONAL STANDARDS FOR PHYSICAL EDUCATION

Standard 1: Demonstrates competency in motor skills and movement patterns needed to perform a variety of physical activities.

Standard 2: Demonstrates understanding of movement concepts, principles, strategies, and tactics as they apply to the learning and performance of physical activities.

Standard 3: Participates regularly in physical activity.

Standard 4: Achieves and maintains a health-enhancing level of physical fitness.

Standard 5: Exhibits responsible personal and social behavior that respects self and others in physical activity settings.

Standard 6: Values physical activity for health, enjoyment, challenge, self-expression, and/or social interaction.

Reprinted from National Association for Sport and Physical Education, 2004, *Moving into the future: National standards for physical education*, 2nd ed. (Reston, VA: NASPE).

Name of event	Targeted dimensions of health	21st century student outcomes	NHE standards	NASPE standards	Page
Beep Baseball			1, 2, 4, 6, 7	1, 2, 5, 6	124
Bowling for Bucks			1, 2, 4, 6, 7	1, 2, 5	98
Cell Phone Recycling			4, 6, 8		38
Cleanup Event			1, 2, 4, 6, 8	5, 6	42
Corporate–Celebrity Fundraiser			4, 5, 6, 8	5, 6	136
Friday Night at the Museum With Chefs' Dinner			4, 5, 6, 8	2, 5, 6	159
Gala			4, 5, 6, 8	2, 5, 6	145

(continued)

(continued)

Name of event	Targeted dimensions of health	21st century student outcomes	NHE standards	NASPE standards	Page
Goalball: Fun for All			1, 2, 4, 6, 7	1, 2, 5	107
Hat Dayz			2, 4, 6, 8	5	31
Ink Cartridge Recycling			4, 6, 8		26
Mini Golf Tournament			4, 5, 6	2, 5, 6	153
Organization Poster			4, 8	6	131
Rubber Duck Race			1, 4, 6, 8	1, 2, 5, 6	70
Scrip Event			4, 8		48

Name of event	Targeted dimensions of health	21st century student outcomes	NHE standards	NASPE standards	Page
Seniors for Seniors: An Evening of Dance			1, 2, 4, 6, 7	1, 2, 5, 6	120
Silent Auction			3, 4, 5, 6, 7, 8	5	83
So You Think You Can Video Dance			1, 4, 5, 6, 7	1, 2, 5, 6	112
Stop, Drop, and Roll Fire Safety Event			1, 4, 5, 7, 8	1, 2, 5, 6	56
Video Game Sport Competition			1, 2, 4, 7, 8	1, 2, 5, 6	102

FUNDRAISING 101

How to plan and implement your fundraiser

This chapter describes the planning, organizing, leading, and evaluating components of fundraising. Also included are strategies for enhancing communication among functional groups during scheduling and implementation periods, which facilitates the achievement of fundraising objectives. Sequencing fundraising activities and developing operational time lines requires communication across functional groups as well as among members of separate fundraising activities. Another key component of fundraising discussed in this chapter is budgeting, which will help you control expenditures and increase profits. Finally, maximizing your fundraising success requires that you find appropriate donors, sponsors, and volunteers for each activity.

FUNDRAISING STEPS

Fundraising can be considered both an art and a science. The art aspect of fundraising refers to the ability to generate interest and produce additional resources through the use of creativity. Although this art aspect is not necessarily crucial for a successful fundraising campaign, it can enhance the bottom line of a fundraising project. It can be described as an innate ability to develop new or better ways to reach fundraising goals. Pooling ideas by brainstorming can increase the level of creativity of any fundraising activity, resulting in greater outcomes as well as a more memorable experience for everyone involved. This section focuses on the scientific process of fundraising—specifically, how to plan, organize, lead, and evaluate a fundraising campaign.

Planning

Before taking any fundraising actions, you need to establish how your profits will be used in the best interest of your organization and stakeholders. When stakeholders have a clear vision of how fundraising profits will be used, they value their own efforts and are better able to sell the events to volunteers and donors. Stakeholders consist of all individuals affected by the fundraising campaign. For instance, donors want to know where money will be used and volunteers want to know that their efforts are for a desirable cause that warrants these resources.

Effective planning, organizing, leading, and evaluating enhance the success of your fundraising endeavors. Part of the planning process is building in the organizing and evaluating functions, which will be discussed later in the chapter. As for the leading function, within the organizing component we will discuss how you can help members become effective leaders. We will begin by discussing the planning component that "encompasses defining an organization's goals, establishing an overall strategy for achieving those goals, and developing a hierarchy of plans to integrate and coordinate activities. It is concerned, then, with ends (what is to be done) as well as with means (how it is to be done)" (Robbins, 1997, p. 130).

As for the science aspect of fundraising, as mentioned previously, fundraising is a step-by-step process that any individual or group of people can use to generate additional resources and achieve objectives. Before learning these steps, however, you need to be aware of the importance of remaining transparent with internal as well as external constituents. Operating in a transparent manner opens communication channels for support, facilitates the achievement of marketing objectives, and creates feedback channels. Transparent communication also creates a culture that encourages stakeholders to address any financial shortcoming.

The steps in the fundraising process are sequential and interdependent. When developing your fundraising plan, determine how much money you hope to raise and your primary donor targets for each activity. Keep in mind that as your plan is implemented, you will find secondary donor targets that will contribute to your bottom line.

The next step in your planning process is to develop a preliminary budget for each fundraising activity; an estimate of the cost of running the event is sufficient. A rule of thumb is that a fundraising budget should not exceed 25 percent of the estimated revenues generated.

The next planning step is prospecting the primary and secondary donor markets. Historical data from previous events can help you with this step, but you must also find new sources for your current and future campaigns. Because developing donor relationships takes time and sensitivity, approach potential donors with the right staff and a sound plan.

Finally, you must establish controls within your fundraising campaign so you can evaluate your progress periodically throughout each fundraising activity. Regular evaluations alert administrators, staff, and volunteers of program needs, tasks that are complete and those that are next in line, as well as the funds received up to that point.

Supporting your fundraising goals by citing research or previous experiences builds a strong case that will help decision makers as well as stakeholders accept your proposal. Stakeholders will also be more likely to put in the effort necessary to achieve the established goals. Citing research and previous experience will also enable you to justify any additional human resources or up-front expenses necessary for launching your project or event.

Setting a time line for every fundraising activity throughout the calendar year is the next step in the planning process. Decision makers need to see time lines, which should include the people assigned to the projects; who are leaders and subordinates; time restraints for certain activities; week-by-week duties and responsibilities; important dates for tasks; the sequence of preevent, event, and postevent duties and responsibilities; and promotions and mediums used for each. Promotion entails what you say in your publicity attempts to create reaction and hopefully further action from your intended audience in some manner. Choosing a vehicle or medium to promote through must also be thoroughly analyzed to ensure it is an appropriate one to enhance your ability to reach the intended audience. Lastly, it is important to remember that promotions are designed specifically for the medium chosen. Communicating with the intended audience through different mediums, such as direct mail, local newspapers, billboards, e-mail blasts, television, radio, and so on requires event staff to develop messages that capture and inform the audience within the limitations of the medium's capability. You also need to establish a system for communicating where the project stands at any given time and ongoing updates of progress toward meeting the financial goal.

Organizing

Organizing your human resources, administrators, staff, and volunteers is essential for facilitating not just each fundraising activity but also your entire campaign of activities. Coordinating multiple events throughout the year is crucial, as is ongoing open communication. Communication will help you identify and solve critical issues, eliminate task duplication, reduce operating costs, and enhance outcomes.

The organizing function involves the arrangement of people and tasks for the purpose of putting plans into action to accomplish goals. Specifically, the steps include dividing tasks, allocating tasks to units and people, coordinating the efforts of units and people, establishing channels of communication, and centralizing or decentralizing decision making. Be sure to assign tasks based on people's specializations and knowledge, skills, and abilities, and to coordinate this work around multiple events throughout the fundraising campaign. By assigning responsibilities according to people's skill sets, you will provide a comfortable yet challenging environment that will help people achieve personal success and maintain high morale.

You need to consider how many activities that require high maintenance by administrators, staff, and volunteers are feasible and plan accordingly. Activities that require advanced levels of knowledge, skills, and abilities can take people away from other projects, which can have a negative impact on the entire fundraising campaign. Include some fundraising activities that can be done by students rather than administrators, staff, and volunteers. Creating a mix of high-, moderate-, and low-maintenance fundraising projects will ensure that your campaign does not crumble like a house of cards and cause negative feedback and publicity.

Keep in mind that your goal is not just fundraising but also developing more informed health-minded people with advanced skill sets for future endeavors. All activities should require student participation to achieve the health dimension learning objectives as well as to enhance the development of 21st century skills. Also, having different target audiences for each fundraising project will keep you from having to approach the same donors and stakeholders, which will reduce the risk of creating animosity toward your organization.

Keep all members of your fundraising project informed about the overriding objectives and why the organization chose to focus on this project. It cannot be overstressed that as these activities come to fruition, the learning objectives tied to each activity must be discussed and evaluated. Learning objectives are a crucial selling tool when seeking approval from decision makers and approaching donors and potential volunteers.

A flow chart is a great tool for organizing various activities for several events over a given period of time (see figure 1.1). A process flow chart shows how the fundraising campaign is performed from start to finish and ensures transparency, keeping all stakeholders informed about the overall project and where it stands in terms of meeting its financial goals. It should identify task administrators and the subordinates under their span of control. A logical method of facilitating the span of control includes type of work being performed as well as the competence of the supervisor and subordinates. Tasks requiring little knowledge, skills, and abilities (KSAs) allow for a wider span of control, while those tasks that require higher levels of KSAs necessitate a narrower span of control. When properly used, a process flow chart improves efficiency and reduces work duplication.

Maintaining a flow chart for all activities can also reveal when certain people are overtaxed or when too many people are assigned to a given project. A flow chart for all activities coded by color is a simple way to keep track of various fundraising projects. Within and across projects, coding staff by the functions performed will help you create a staff schedule to maintain progress. An additional benefit of the process flow chart is that it facilitates communication within each fundraising project as well as across projects.

Time line

Fundraising Campaign Agenda and Processes

September

Health and Wellness (H and W) Committee meets to plan fundraising campaign activities.
H and W Committee creates subcommittees to spearhead fundraising activities.
H and W subcommittees further develop separate fundraising activity proposals, which includes potential locations, human resource needs, tentative budget, time line, and learning objectives.

October

H and W Committee meets to review and confirm proposals.
H and W Committee finalizes fundraising campaign and submits proposals for PTA review.

November

H and W Committee meets with PTA after review and moves forward with approved activities.
With plans established and approved, H and W Committee must organize human resources for the functions of each activity.

Time line

Seniors Dance Event Agenda and Processes

December

- Meet with the seniors of the school to discuss the event procedures.
- Research senior centers, retirement homes, assisted living homes, YMCAs, and so on by using Internet search engines and local phone books.
- Create a poll to inquire what types of dance styles and classes adults and seniors prefer using Microsoft Word. This is a survey that will ask the adults and seniors questions (e.g., What is your favorite style of dance to watch? What is your favorite style of dance to perform? What kind of dance class have you always wanted to take?).
- Distribute polls to the parents of the students and to different centers by hand delivering or mailing them from the main office.

January

- Collect polls by hand or by mail to determine what classes to teach for the fundraiser.
- Research dance styles using your school library, public library, and Internet search engines.
- Plan for practice time in physical education class, in lunch, after school, or in free periods during school hours with the other dance instructor students.

January and February

- Students will create a flyer for the fundraiser using Microsoft Publisher. The flyer will include a description of the event, date, time, donation information, reception to follow, and pictures of the dance styles.
- Distribute the flyer to the researched centers by mail or by hand and distribute the flyer to your parents and grandparents by hand.
- Brainstorm together in class (e.g., other ways to make money, raffle prizes).

February and March

- Collect raffle prizes by asking stores or family members to donate items.
- Students will choose lead instructors for each style of dance.
- Students will help each other plan the choreography and steps for class by meeting during or after school.
- Students will decide on their food and drink contribution for the reception after the fundraiser.
- Students will make poster boards for raffle prizes that will include the types of raffles and price of the raffle tickets.
- Select a musical playlist for each class and bring in copies of any music you have to add to the playlist.
- Choose jobs for the day of the event including money collector, music assistant, water seller, and address taker.
- Create a blank list for participants' addresses. The list will be a table with the participant's name, home address, and donation amount made in Microsoft Word.
- Purchase or make food and drinks for the reception.

Figure 1.1a Fundraising process flow chart showing the agenda and processes of a seniors dance event.

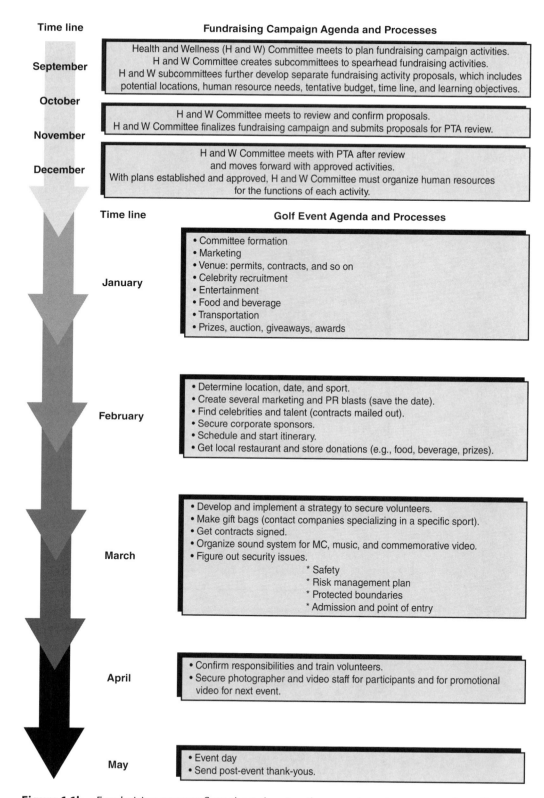

Time line   **Fundraising Campaign Agenda and Processes**

September

Health and Wellness (H and W) Committee meets to plan fundraising campaign activities.
H and W Committee creates subcommittees to spearhead fundraising activities.
H and W subcommittees further develop separate fundraising activity proposals, which includes
potential locations, human resource needs, tentative budget, time line, and learning objectives.

October

November

H and W Committee meets to review and confirm proposals.
H and W Committee finalizes fundraising campaign and submits proposals for PTA review.

December

H and W Committee meets with PTA after review
and moves forward with approved activities.
With plans established and approved, H and W Committee must organize human resources
for the functions of each activity.

Time line   **Golf Event Agenda and Processes**

January

- Committee formation
- Marketing
- Venue: permits, contracts, and so on
- Celebrity recruitment
- Entertainment
- Food and beverage
- Transportation
- Prizes, auction, giveaways, awards

February

- Determine location, date, and sport.
- Create several marketing and PR blasts (save the date).
- Find celebrities and talent (contracts mailed out).
- Secure corporate sponsors.
- Schedule and start itinerary.
- Get local restaurant and store donations (e.g., food, beverage, prizes).

March

- Develop and implement a strategy to secure volunteers.
- Make gift bags (contact companies specializing in a specific sport).
- Get contracts signed.
- Organize sound system for MC, music, and commemorative video.
- Figure out security issues.
  - * Safety
  - * Risk management plan
  - * Protected boundaries
  - * Admission and point of entry

April

- Confirm responsibilities and train volunteers.
- Secure photographer and video staff for participants and for promotional video for next event.

May

- Event day
- Send post-event thank-yous.

Figure 1.1b Fundraising process flow chart showing the agenda and processes of a golf event.

Leading

The leading function is action oriented: it involves the execution of the established fundraising plans. Leading includes delegating, managing in a changing environment, motivating people, and managing diverse situations. As a leader, you must keep people on task by organizing the structure of the program. This structure, which is explained in the organizing section, essentially requires a detailed breakdown of duties and responsibilities along with a time line for achieving goals. A transparent and detailed plan keeps people aware of their specific tasks and gives them more independence to operate and perform the functions assigned to them.

Directing people is your primary responsibility as a leader. This involves choosing people with the knowledge base, skills, and abilities needed for completing tasks. You will need a thorough understanding of project needs and the people available, as well as good decision-making skills. Delegating is an important skill and hard to acquire; the ability to delegate can either make or break a fundraising event. The importance of delegating is clear: because you cannot do everything by yourself, choosing the right people for the tasks at hand ensures a successful undertaking.

Another key component of project leadership is the ability to adapt on the fly and recreate goals and objectives if necessary. Establishing an effective evaluation system during the planning process will help you react to the current situation appropriately. Evaluation will be discussed further in the next section, but must be mentioned here to help you understand your leadership role. As the overseer of all aspects of your fundraising projects, you must measure progress and compare it to predetermined standards so you can determine whether to continue as planned or adjust your strategies and tactics.

Evaluating

The primary purpose of evaluating is to measure your progress toward your fundraising goals. Putting in controls to measure against during the project time line will help you determine whether adjustments are necessary. Controls are basically how far along the staff has come to completing certain tasks or how much money has been raised at a certain point of the campaign. Knowing your progress will also enable you to let all stakeholders know whether they are ahead, on target, or behind in achieving their monetary goals.

Some of the major areas to evaluate are money raised, in-kind donations, human resource allocation, tactics implemented, strategy focus, prospecting of volunteers and donors, and budget. Knowing where you stand in these areas will help you make any managerial adjustments needed.

Evaluating project staff will help you motivate them to attain their goals. Positive feedback shows them that their vision is close to coming to fruition.

BUDGETING

When planning a fundraising event, an essential element to consider is budgeting. For those new to the process, a budget is simply a quantified, planned financial course of action over a period of time. It attempts to estimate costs and revenues.

Creating a working budget for a fundraising event is important for many reasons. First, it forces you to consider the expected demand for your products and services. Considering demand makes you aware of the resources you need to meet your goals. Budgeting for fundraising events also highlights problems you may face in meeting your goals and allows for sufficient time to correct the deficiencies. Lastly, budgeting creates a standard against which results can be compared and is vital for event evaluation (Gordon, Hilton, & Welsch, 1988).

A thorough budget must be developed prior to approving the event and must include both operating and material costs. Operating costs include the cost of staff, sales expenses (e.g., automobile gas, telephone usage), and administrative tasks such as choosing the fundraising activity, developing the proposal, implementing the activity, evaluating the project outcome, and reporting the outcomes to the organization. People taking on administrative or coordinative roles will need time to develop and implement the project. They will also spend many hours coordinating and leading staff. Each event requires a committed administrative staff and at times their efforts may require a financial reward. At other times, these administrators are offering in-kind assistance, which is their way of donating to the fundraising campaign. So make sure during the planning stage to address what costs will be levied by any administrators.

Materials are the other regular budget item for fundraising projects. Costs that typically fall under the materials category include stationery supplies, mailings, copying expenses, phone calls, gas for transportation, web page design and maintenance, up-front cost for products used in the activity, advertising or promotion fees, and electricity. These line items differ depending on the activity, but generally will be your primary financial concerns. Insurance policies are required for some activities.

You need to be as thorough as possible with your fundraising budget: it should show all sources and quantities of cash flow expected for each event. The budgeting process can be broken into the following seven simple steps (Vohwinkle, n.d.):

1. **Gather every financial statement you can.** This generally includes bank statements, recent bills, and any other information regarding past sources of income and expenses. The main purpose of gathering this information is to compile averages from prior events and to use them as a basis for evaluation.

2. **Record all sources of income.** Compile all sources and quantities of income expected from an event including all revenue sources as well as interest income from notes, debt recoveries, and credit saves. This revenue budget

is simply a forecast because it is based on projections of future sales rather than known, substantial figures. When compiling a revenue budget, take into consideration your competitors, advertising budget, sales force effectiveness, and other relevant factors. From the various projections assembled, attempt to select the most feasible price to charge your consumers for your event.

3. **Create a list of expenses for events.** Compile all sources and quantities of expenses from a future event including wages for employees as well as the costs of utilities, entertainment, promotions, data processing, and miscellaneous items. Expense budgets list the primary activities undertaken and assign monetary amounts to each of them. When compiling expense budgets, pay particular attention to the fixed expenses as addressed in step 4.

4. **Separate expenses into two categories (fixed and variable).** Fixed expenses are those that are required for each event and remain stable from event to event. They are essential to the budgeting process and are very unlikely to change. A good example of a fixed expense is utilities. Variable expenses, on the other hand, fluctuate greatly depending on the event and include categories such as labor wages, entertainment, and promotional fees.

5. **Total your income and expenses for each event.** If your calculation shows more income than expenses, the event is off to a good start. You can disburse the excess income to other areas of the budget. If, however, there is a higher expense column, you will need to make some changes.

6. **Make adjustments to expenses.** If expenses are higher than income, search through your variable expenses for the discrepancy and look for possible areas in which to cut back. It is much easier to cut variable expenses than it is to cut fixed expenses because variable expenses are generally nonrecurring.

7. **Review your budget frequently.** Budget reviews should be conducted often to compare projections to actual outcome. They will show where you did well and where you need to improve for the next event.

When formulating budgets for fundraising events, a preliminary budget may be superseded by the actual budget. A preliminary budget is a premature estimate of the total time and funds required for the event. The final budget will be a precise financial evaluation of your fundraising campaign to use for future similar events. It is always good to see a final budget that shows lower expenses than the preliminary budget (Levine, 2001).

SECURING VOLUNTEERS AND DONORS

One of the most important tasks in a fundraising campaign is identifying primary and secondary markets of donors and volunteers. A plan for securing volunteers and how they will be used is essential to the success of the entire campaign. Although the desired result is financial inputs to meet a predetermined goal, we cannot overstress the importance of locating and securing enough volunteers to implement your fundraising campaign. *Prospecting* is a term used to describe the process of seeking donors and volunteers. The prospecting of each group is discussed separately in this section because what you are prospecting for from each group is unique.

Donors differ depending on the fundraising activity. If you choose to focus your activities on societal health issues, you can identify stakeholders who are closely aligned with those issues. These constituents have a vested interest so they are prone to contribute either in-kind or monetarily. In-kind donations include human resources, products, equipment, or marketing or promotional support. In-kind donations should eventually generate revenues, either directly or indirectly. For example, in-kind product donations can be sold to donors or participants of the fundraising activity; in-kind human resources expertise or equipment can extend the reach of the event or facilitate the process to make the project more efficient, thereby increasing revenues or decreasing operating costs. Prospecting for closely aligned constituents, individuals, or groups can be done by researching historical data from previous events, community-based groups or associations such as the Veterans of Foreign Wars (VFW) in the United States, or the local chamber of commerce. This is not an all-inclusive list but just a prospecting starting point.

Knowing who to target as potential volunteers for your fundraising activity is crucial. It is extremely important to understand the level of knowledge, skills, and abilities (KSAs) required to perform the various tasks of your fundraising activities. Determine the knowledge volunteers will need and the skill set necessary for achieving project tasks. You will also need to evaluate potential volunteers' ability to perform the necessary tasks at the present time.

Prior to moving forward with any fundraising activity, you need to determine whether you have the KSAs internally or need to seek help from outside your organization. What are the chances of securing outside volunteers? As mentioned earlier, in-kind donations of expertise to address a shortcoming of internal KSAs can ensure the success of your fundraising event.

CONCLUSION

Although fundraising generally delivers some results, this book will help you increase your fundraising profits. As the leader of your campaign, you are directly responsible for communicating about the events as well as coordinating the evaluations to ensure progress. The step-by-step process laid out in this chapter will help you reach your goals in a more straightforward manner. A recognition of the interdependence of the stages of fundraising will help you evaluate your project's progress so you can determine whether to continue forward or modify the original plan to ensure success. Finally, because believing in the importance of your fundraising project makes it that much easier to sell it to all constituents, choose your events wisely.

EXTENDING YOUR FUNDRAISING POTENTIAL

Social networking, donation networking, and grant writing

Modern times call for modern solutions. Therefore, it behooves us to take a close look at technology and its fundraising applications. To be successful, fundraising efforts must be creative, innovative, inexpensive, and considerably more sophisticated than they were a generation ago. Rapidly evolving communication and technology tools continue to change the ways we interact and work with each other. Organizations must keep pace with contemporary methods to best meet the needs of those they serve. Our society is becoming increasingly dependent on the Internet. This is good news for fundraisers. If the goal is to reach both previous supporters and new audiences, technology in general—and social networking sites in particular—offer an incredibly powerful and effective means of doing so. We have at our disposal free, invaluable tools for selling products and ideas and raising funds for our local communities.

SOCIAL NETWORKING

Social networks offer an eco-friendly, prevalent, and popular way to communicate information and to expand your community. Today's young people face unprecedented pressure as they prepare to compete in the global market. Technology constantly redefines the essential skills our youth need to succeed in the 21st century. Educators and leaders alike must embrace and befriend all of the tools available to them—including social networks—as they mentor students and role model behaviors that empower them to become responsible, productive citizens of the world. With effective preparation, educators and interested community members can communicate freely, thereby raising funds, generating awareness and involvement, and cultivating engagement.

Social networking connects millions of subscribers (and target groups) virtually with families, friends, and coworkers, wherever they might be. A social network is a specialized website, or forum, through which individuals, groups, and organizations can share, learn, disseminate information, and discuss common interests. At present, there are hundreds of social networking sites, and that number changes constantly.

Some of the most recognized social networking sites currently are MySpace, Facebook, YouTube, Twitter, and Flickr. Each offers a place to connect with people, but maintains its own unique characteristics. MySpace, which has been popular with high school-aged students, for example, gives people the opportunity to create their own pages, invite friends, and post almost anything digitally on their page. YouTube provides the opportunity to post homemade videos. Facebook promotes reconnecting with old friends, and Twitter is a microblogging site that allows only short, text-based messages (although users can quickly build large networks of followers). Blogs ("web logs"), also a form of social networking, are often linked through RSS (Really Simple Syndication) feeds.

One significant development in fundraising is SMS, or text message, fundraising. This method was debuted during U.S. president Barack Obama's presidential campaign and subsequent worldwide disaster relief efforts following an earthquake in Haiti. However, this form of fundraising has yet to be used in a long-term capacity.

Regardless of the selection of or rationale for choosing a particular connection, social networks open up lines of communication. Some sites may have more merit or value than others (see the section on Facebook), but the bottom line is that any of these digital online tools can establish, maintain, and cultivate vibrant networks of people. With planning and organization, these networks, in turn, can help support your organization's financial needs. We suggest that organizations use a combination of these tools year-round to cultivate a community of interested followers and build awareness for fundraising events.

Once registered as part of an online community on a networking site, community members can exchange information, support each other in their common interests, assess and discuss the strategy of the event being promoted, and most important, build awareness for upcoming fundraising events. A leader of your organization should monitor and update the site daily, but with this system, the organization can present important information and new events to the whole community at one time: families, educators, volunteer and community-based organizations, faith communities, health care institutions and providers, and government and media organizations. Additionally, existing followers can be reminded to connect with their friends, which expands the community that uses the networking site. Because social networks are often connected to mobile devices, they can offer communication that is instant and effortless.

Facebook

Facebook, founded in 2004, is free to users. It is one of the most popular social networking websites in the world, boasts hundreds of millions of active users, and facilitates communication in what it describes as a "trusted environment". Clearly, this presents an undeniable opportunity for organizations to raise awareness, network with potential volunteers and donors, and solicit funds from local community members and businesses and other local Facebook users.

An important thing to remember about Facebook is that it is a social network of friends that reflects real life. A Facebook friend list, then, can be a mixture of people with interest in your activity, including friends, students, parents, boosters, coworkers, peers, neighbors, and family members. The idea behind social networking is connecting groups of friends to increase awareness of your event among people with similar interests.

Social media can create a robust, dynamic, and collaborative forum within your organization and cultivate a community that has no physical boundaries. Your organization's fundraisers can learn how to cultivate a community while expanding awareness of the organization and related fundraising events. Once you are connected, you need to ensure a consistent flow of relevant information about your organization, participants, and other events.

In these economically challenging times, many organizations have fewer resources and therefore need community-building strategies. Facebook is a free, popular online tool that can help you create conversations about, drive awareness of, and raise money for your fundraising activities.

The activity at the end of this chapter shows how you can use Facebook to extend your fundraising efforts by building a fan page for people who are interested in your organization, your events, and your fundraising goals. Keep in mind that you are always looking to expand connections to new people that can help your organization in some way.

Getting visitors to "like" or visit your fan page can be accomplished by promoting it to everyone who is connected to any member of your organization on Facebook. Once people "like" your group's page, it shows on their own page where their friends can see it and perhaps become interested in your community or fundraising event.

Once you have created your fan page, an adult leader must commit time to overseeing and monitoring the discussions to ensure that communication runs freely and appropriately. That person also needs to continually maintain the page to ensure a connection between your organization and its followers. A fan page can include a monthly newsletter, discount vouchers, contests, links, polls, free tickets, and question-and-answer sessions. It can also seamlessly stream blog posts and post tutorial videos from interesting leaders at your organization. Offering tutorials or discussing hot topics that relate to your page is a way to expand your community.

As your community of followers gets larger, your page becomes an effective way to disseminate information. Facebook fan pages allow you to message your fans all at once. Remember to add your Facebook fan page to e-mail signatures, business cards, and anywhere contact information is provided.

Blogging and Twitter

Organizations across the country use blogging to keep website viewers informed about current or upcoming events, fundraisers, and anecdotes to strengthen their connection to the organization. You may want to subscribe to a web-based aggregator service (we suggest Google Reader) that can "push" information to you every time a post is made to websites you are interested in. One can choose to read blogs to remain up to date on current issues that impact their group in some way. This information can be reframed or reposted to the social networking site which can engage followers further.

The latest movement in the blogosphere is microblogging, which occurs most often through the popular website Twitter. The concept behind Twitter (and similar microblogging sites) is real-time information networking. It enables organizations to stay connected to and engaged with a community of followers and share limited information quickly, obtain feedback, and build virtual relationships with potential or future supporters. Twitter represents the opportunity to exchange information in real time. Often, groups post important updates on Twitter so followers are connected to events as they occur. This enhances awareness as well as engagement for the followers whether they are attending the event or just interested in its success.

Like Facebook, Twitter facilitates the cultivation of a community of followers. Using Twitter or Facebook, you can send messages that advertise events or alert followers to what is happening at your organization at that exact moment!

Bookmarking

Social bookmarking services can be used to bookmark valuable Internet resources for later recovery (we recommend Delicious). With Delicious, you can save, manage, and share pages with others in a central area on the Internet. With a little bit of planning, sites such as Delicious bring a powerful community aspect to social bookmarking, just as Facebook and Twitter do for social networking, by connecting people to others with the same interests. Social bookmarking sites allow you to contact others with similar interests or backgrounds through comments, e-mail, or instant message. In this way you can build a relationship, expand your personal learning network, and transform your learning experience. Social bookmarking sites also facilitate collaborations among people at anytime and anyplace in the world.

Social bookmarking sites connect people through the use of keywords and tags. Keywords and tags are words used to define the concept being examined. They are used to provide reasoning and logic so that others can link to the same concept. These can be used to identify more content about similar topics to create shared links that can be accessed by anyone in a given network.

DONATION NETWORKING

As discussed, any fundraising organization can benefit from a well-organized plan that involves free online tools. One such tool is donation and charity mall websites, which are viable, low-cost Internet fundraising tools. As with Facebook, however, someone (we suggest an adult leader) must set up a basic web page for the group and monitor it.

A donation or charity mall site allows registered organizations to receive a percentage of the purchases made on the site. Some charity malls specialize in schools and school-related groups, (e.g., One Cause at www.onecause.com/causes), similar to the program Box Tops for Education. The entire structure is built on commission. Some websites, such as Bidding for Good (www.biddingforgood.com/online-auction-services) and iGive (www.igive.com), offer online auction fundraisers. Other sites are not affiliated with shopping or auctions and simply accept donations for a cause. Following are some examples:

◆ **Donors Choose** (www.donorschoose.org). School project requests are posted on the site, and donors can browse and give any amount to the project of their choosing. Once the project meets the desired funding goal, the materials are sent to the school. Donors receive photos of the project, thank-you letters, and a cost report detailing how the donation was spent.

◆ **ChipIn** (www.chipin.com). At this site, groups describe the project they are collecting money for, the amount they want to raise, and the date by which the funds are required. A ChipIn Widget, or application, that can be installed and completed within a web page (groupname.chipin.com) is embedded on the group's favorite social networking sites, and funds are collected via PayPal.

◆ **Crowdrise** (www.crowdrise.com). This site is a compilation of crowdsourcing, social networking, incentives, and more. Crowdsourcing or crowdfunding are terms used to describe openly calling upon a group of people or a community to carry out a request, perform a task, or solve a problem. Like Facebook, a designee from the group signs up for a charitable profile page. Next, the group starts a fundraising campaign by setting up a project page on the website. The share button on the project page is used to message people using e-mail, Facebook, Twitter, or a combination.

Regardless of the social network(s) your group chooses to use, when constructing your online fundraising project sites, you may want to consider the following (Kirkwood, 2010):

◆ **Make personal contacts.** Directly invite people who have an affiliation with the group's members or governing body whenever possible. Mass or generic postings, tweets, or e-mails can be used to reach a larger audience; however, they can lack a personal tone that makes people feel connected to the group or the goal of the project.

◆ **Narrate your cause.** Describe the project and how it will affect those who will benefit from the funding in detail. Share the meaningfulness of the project and how contributing financially or as a volunteer can make a difference in the lives of others. Describe personal experiences and events that led up to the development of the project, and offer comments from students or community members.

◆ **Be realistic and relevant.** Describe an attainable goal that includes the allocation of funds. Clear and in-depth descriptions instill confidence that you will have a successful outcome. Be creative in your attempts to reach contributors, but provide an easy way to make a simple and immediate donation. Effortlessness is an important aspect of online donations. You can also provide choices (e.g., small, noninvolved commitments or larger, more involved commitments) so participants can choose what works best for them.

◆ **Be professional.** A well-organized and error-free site is appreciated by the people navigating it and, therefore, can increase the likelihood of contributions. Donors who receive reports of the results of the project may be more inclined to donate again. It is also important to thank and otherwise recognize those that have donated in any possible way.

GRANTS

Grants can be another source of money for your organization. By definition, grants are gifts of money, goods, or services. Grant writing takes time and effort; however, the benefits can certainly outweigh the cost. There are many choices and many ways grants can be used based on the goal(s) of the group. Grants are typically given to fund specific projects and usually require awardees to follow suggested or required guidelines regarding project implementation and the reporting of outcomes. The grant process begins with submitting a proposal that is obtained either by personal request or by a publicized offering. The application is then reviewed by the grant agency. Grants are issued by government, public, and private organizations, foundations, and institutes. Grant fund seeking starts with identifying a need and then investigating grant sources that may fund that need.

Identifying Needs and Funding Sources

The first stage of securing a grant is forming a research team or designating someone to research and present a list of grants to a grant team for further prioritizing. Collaborations will bring in people with expertise in certain areas and quicken the grant writing process. People with researching, writing, proofreading, and word processing skills would be helpful. Sharing the workload makes the process more manageable and also increases the chance of success because the proposal is reviewed by a number of people prior to submission.

The list of grant resources is ever changing. Following is a sampling:

Digital Wish: www.digitalwish.com/dw/digitalwish/grant_awards

Head Start Body Start: www.aahperd.org/headstartbodystart/grants/

Physical Education Program (PEP) Grant: www.aahperd.org/naspe/about/announcements/PEP_Announced.cfm

Sprint Character Ed: www.sprint.com/responsibility/education/character/

Keep Gym in School: www.keepgyminschool.com/

Run for Something Better: www.aahperd.org/naspe/grants/grants/ING/index.cfm?cid=00001

Run for Good: www.sauconyrunforgood.com/

ING Unsung Heroes: www.ing-usa.com/us/aboutING/CorporateCitizenship/Education/INGUnsungHeroes/index.htm

LEGO Children's Fund: www.legochildrensfund.org/Guidelines.html

Baseball Tomorrow: http://mlb.mlb.com/mlb/official_info/community/btf.jsp?content=about

Once you have selected a group of grants, you must narrow your list by determining your group's qualifications based on any restrictions or rules. Following is a list of questions to ask during the research, reviewing, and narrowing stage of your grant writing project:

- What types of projects do they fund or not fund?
- Who were past awardees of this grant? Is there an abstract or sample project from past winners?
- What are the application requirements and guidelines? Are there specific criteria that must be addressed? (You must follow the directions very carefully because you will be rejected if you do not meet the granting agency's specific guidelines.)
- Is there a contact e-mail address or phone number for questions that may arise?
- What is the deadline? Will we be able to complete the proposal in time?

Grant Writing 101

When formulating your reason for requesting a grant, consider the results of your project and how it will affect the recipients. Instead of focusing on what you will do with the grant, focus on how the grant will influence the lives of the children or recipients. Begin by presenting a particular goal based on a problem for which you have a practical solution. You may want to include comments or a testimonial about the project from an administrator or community member. How does your project expand on something already existing or create something completely new or different? Distinctiveness will catch the attention of the grant reviewers. How will students or recipients be involved? Describe how they will participate in the application process and the actual project (e.g., name it or design the logo). Describe in detail how the solution will be accomplished and any research that testifies to the success.

You may also need to think about alternative funding sources to help you reach your goal. The grant you are applying for may satisfy only part of your overall project, and you may need to seek funding from other sources.

As you write your grant, make sure that your need, goals, solutions, and assessments are interconnected and mutually supportive. Because every grant is unique, a general list of concrete steps is not appropriate. However, the following writing strategies can help:

- Be specific in your implementation plans.
- Detail how recipients will be involved and educational benchmarks will be addressed.
- Describe community connections or affiliations and how they will be included.
- Demonstrate a clear vision, and follow the guidelines provided.
- Explain a scenario or situation that will take place during implementation.
- Convey the impact of the project on all those involved, both directly and indirectly.
- Share youngsters' reflections or comments from community members as supplements.
- Involve students or recipients in the entire process, from grant writing to creating assessment reports.
- Make sure your writing is clear, concise, and free of errors; use lists where appropriate.
- Provide examples of other projects, offer a history of successes, and detail the expertise and achievements of those who will be involved.
- Stress the need for the grant, and use research to back up your claims.
- Invite people with varying backgrounds to review the proposal and application.

Creating and Maintaining a Facebook Page

Activity Description

Many people, including celebrities, politicians, professional athletes, and businesses, use Facebook fan pages because they are easy to set up and facilitate easy conversations and interactions with friends, communities, and in some cases, actual fans. Because of the proliferation of Facebook, most people are familiar with fan pages. When managed well, they build awareness for your group's activities and fundraising needs.

Ideally, your fundraising group should put together a fundraising calendar at the beginning of the school year or fundraising season so that all of your group's members know the timing of the events. Once that information is compiled, a Facebook fan page is a great way to make people aware of your events from beginning to end! Followers, administrators, and community members can comment, post photographs and videos, and spread the word about the purpose of the event, the people involved, and the potential for fun.

Facebook requires that every fan page be linked to a Facebook personal profile. Because of the popularity of Facebook, there shouldn't be a problem finding an adult leader within your organizational committee willing to link your fundraising group's fan page to his or her personal profile. This person is the primary administrator and should assign secondary administrators who can also control the page to ensure that it remains active.

Because most young people have well-developed Facebook communities, they can help with outreach by "liking" the fan page. Often, young people have legions of friends, which can help expand the community. This reveals the fan page on their profiles, where it will be seen by their Facebook friends, who may themselves choose to "like" it. In this way, awareness of your fundraising group and each fundraising event grows exponentially! A fan page that is continually maintained and shared by people who "like" it creates a perpetual connection between your group and interested people.

Educational Objectives

Students will:

- Develop an increased sense of global awareness and increase their financial, economic, and entrepreneurial literacy.
- Increase their health and environmental literacy as the group organizes environmental friendly and socially responsible events.
- Increase their innovation skills by focusing on creativity, communication, and collaboration with a variety of constituencies as the group organizes environmental friendly and socially responsible events.
- Be exposed to the complexities of a work environment and use problem-solving skills as the group organizes environmental friendly and socially responsible events.

Adults will:

- Create a functional and viable marketing strategy that will teach students life lessons such as social skills, team building, productivity, accountability, and leadership.

The community will:

- Benefit from local organizations teaching the skills young people need to be productive and socially responsible citizens in today's challenging world.
- Benefit from adults modeling socially responsible behavior.

Targeted Dimensions of Health

| Social | Mental | Emotional | Environmental |

Standards Met

National Health Education standards 3, 4, 5, 6, 7, and 8
21st century student outcomes:

Life and Career Skills   **Learning and Innovation Skills**   **Information, Media, and Technology Skills**

21st century interdisciplinary themes: Global awareness; financial, economic, business, and entrepreneurial literacy; civic literacy; health literacy; environmental literacy

Age Level

A Facebook fan page for fundraising should be created and administered by adults. Involvement, engagement, and commenting can be performed by anyone with a Facebook account.

Human Resources Requirements

Low to moderate levels of knowledge, skills, and ability are necessary to create and monitor the fan page. Adult administrators need to be in touch with those who are planning the fundraising events. It would be helpful to have an adult photographer and videographer involved so that the fan page can be full of media-rich content.

Recommended Procedures

1. Meet with like-minded, interested community members to form a fundraising group.
2. Identify your monetary goals for fundraising.
3. Create and finalize a 12-month fundraising calendar.
4. Identify a primary Facebook fan page administrator and two or three secondary administrators.

5. Identify a group photographer (short videos are a great idea, too).
6. Identify a photography editor.
7. Post your fundraising goal and calendar of events on your fan page.
8. Create signage for advertising your fan page, and encourage students, parents, and community members to "like" your fan page.
9. Have the organization's administrators advertise your fan page consistently throughout the year. Seek opportunities to remind the community to "like" your fan page. Sporting events, programs, plays, and assemblies are all opportunities to advertise and promote your fan page. The more people who "like" your fan page, the more people your group can communicate to freely.

Event Preparation Time Line

This time line provides guidelines for organizing a social network starting at the beginning of the school year or fundraising season.

Beginning of the School Year or Fundraising Season: Create a Facebook Fan Page

There is an assumption here that you have already created a calendar of fundraising events and designated an adult administrator and two or three assistant administrators.

One of the fastest ways to create a fan page is to search for one that has already been created. Scroll down to the bottom left corner of this page and click on the link that says "Create a Page." We suggest you choose "Official Page" and then designate "Brand, Product, Organization" and use the drop-down menu to select "Nonprofit." We suggest that you provide the name of your organization (e.g., ABC School Booster Club) and choose a memorable yet easy-to-understand name. Because there is the potential for many fundraising events in one year, we suggest that you cultivate one page for all fundraising events for the organization, because you can't change it once you finalize the fan page. When you have carefully created a viable fan page name and confirmed that you have the authorization to create this page, click on the button "Create Official Page."

Facebook allows administrators to configure a lot of settings. Be certain to spend some time establishing these settings to ensure that your page meets the needs of your group. To begin, you will notice a "Like Box" (be certain to "like" your own page). You will also see four tabs across the page: "Get Started," "Wall," "Info," "Photos," and "Discussion." Begin with "Get Started" and take the time to insert information consistently in all of these tabs.

The key to setting up a fan page is getting others who use Facebook to "like" your fan page. The "Like Box" connects people to your group! The more people who connect to your fan page, the more people who connect to your group's cause! Facebook provides the structure for you to create this page, but your administrator must upload and monitor the content on this page. Remember, if you want fans, you have to let people know your group is on Facebook. Put an icon or link everywhere you communicate with interested people—newsletters, business cards, posters, signs, websites, and blogs—everywhere.

Get Started

Once you've clicked on the "Get Started" tab, upload an appropriate photo. We suggest that you upload a photo right away to your page. Your first photo will be the one that everyone sees when viewing the fan page, so choose wisely.

Invite Your Friends

Click on the blue "Invite Your Friends" button to reveal a list of potential friends. To invite a friend to "like" your fan page, simply click on the friend's picture. You can invite as many friends as you want. When you are finished, click the blue button at the bottom that says "Send Invitation." We suggest that you attach a personal message with your invitation to draw people in. The hope here is that those who "like" your fan page will also invite their friends and the word will spread (you may also want to remind your followers to invite their friends at a later date!).

Tell Your Fans

In the "Tell Your Friends" area, Facebook guides you to "Find Your Web E-mail Contacts" on Hotmail, Gmail, Yahoo, and other sites. This feature facilitates a painless search of your current e-mail contacts to find people who may be interested in your group's fan page. This is the fastest and easiest way to find potential fans. Again, the hope here is that those who "like" your fan page will also invite their e-mail contacts to "like" your fan page. That joins everyone in a network of people interested in your activity (again, you may also want to remind your followers to invite their e-mail contacts at a later date).

Post Status Updates

Status updates allow you to share information with your audience (i.e., everybody who has "liked" your page). We suggest that you post important information here so that your audience is kept aware of your group's needs, events, or successes. The more frequently you post information here, the more information your community receives.

Wall Posts

The wall of your fan page is a place for fans to post comments, photos, links, and videos. Encouraging your audience to add information here develops your community by enhancing everyone's involvement.

Info

The info section of your fan page is where you articulate some basic, detailed, and contact information. Here you can have a clickable web address, organizational overview, mission, and available products.

Photos

The fan page has a section to display photos. Members of your community will enjoy seeing the visual summaries of your events and will recognize various people who contributed to the events. A tag connects a person, page, or place to something that is posted. Continually updating and tagging increases awareness of your group's events. Every time a tag is applied, the person who is tagged is notified about it. A variety of photo albums of individual fundraising events can be added at any time. Over time, this provides a valuable record and visual reference for the many positive events your organizations holds. Plus it's another way to engage the community of followers in your group.

Discussion

In the discussion section of your page, post hot topics, or ask questions to encourage fans of your page to comment and become more engaged with your events.

One Month Prior to the Fundraising Event

- Post status updates to make your audience aware of any needs your group may have. Continue to cultivate awareness of your event and articulate your fundraising goals.
- Continue to remind people to "like" your fan page.

During Every Fundraising Event

- Designate a member to post status updates continually during the event. Try to keep your audience (those who have "liked" your page) up to date on everything that is happening throughout the event.
- Take photographs and videos to upload at a later date. These should attempt to capture all of the participants of the event including adults, students, volunteers, and participants. The more fun-filled photos, the better! It is a great idea to post pictures, videos, comments as the event is occurring, too.

After the Fundraising Event

- Post status updates about the successes of your event.
- Create a photo album on the fan page and upload photos and videos (with tags) to it.
- Begin to post information about your upcoming fundraising event.

CONCLUSION

A variety of social media platforms are available for building relationships and sharing information with others. Although Facebook, Twitter, and Delicious are the most popular at the time of this book's printing, other social networking sites and tools should not be ignored. We suggest that you begin by organizing and reviewing connections to community members through popular social networks because of the potential to extend your group's fundraising efforts.

LOW-LEVEL FUNDRAISERS

Require little maintenance and are short in duration

The activities in this chapter are regarded as low-level knowledge, skills, and abilities fundraisers. This means that most of them require resources that are readily available to most organizations. Much of the required work can be done by adult supervisors or competent volunteers. This is not to say that some of the tasks are not involved; however, most can be carried out by properly directed youngsters and adult volunteers.

The ink cartridge recycling activity is presented first because it is the easiest to implement and can yield a sizable profit. As the chapter progresses, the activities become more labor intensive, although they build on the skills and exercises used in previous activities. The stop, drop, and roll fire safety fundraiser is more difficult to organize than others are, but it relies on skills that most adults have: a basic knowledge of the computer, the ability to perform web searches for additional resources, the ability to network within the community, and moderate supervisory skills.

Ink Cartridge Recycling

Activity Description

This activity will not only raise a low to moderate level of funds but also benefit the environment and teach young people their role in protecting the world they live in. Millions of ink cartridges are thrown away every day, and several cups of oil are required to produce new ink cartridges from scratch. Refunds for used cartridges can range from a few cents to as much as $3 depending on the brand and ink color. A simple web search will identify where your group can turn in used ink cartridges. Most large chain business supply stores accept used cartridges and offer remuneration in the form of gift cards or cash rewards. Independent companies also found on the web offer cash or checks for your used cartridges.

This activity involves low-level knowledge, skills, and abilities on the part of young participants and adult leaders. It is a great beginner project and can be run concurrently with other fundraising projects.

Educational Objectives

Students will:

- Understand the impact of recycling and reusing everyday materials.
- Create their own announcements soliciting empty ink cartridges from their neighbors.
- Interact and communicate with others (neighbors and other students).
- Set and meet individual performance goals, and demonstrate productivity and accountability (i.e., when creating and distributing flyers and collecting used cartridges).

Adults will:

- Mobilize students and organize their efforts with minimal hands-on time.
- Model socially responsible behavior as well as environmental literacy.

The community will:

- Benefit from the interest of local citizens in maintaining the integrity of the environment.
- Experience increased cohesiveness from citizens working together.

Targeted Dimensions of Health

Social   **Mental**   **Emotional**   **Environmental**

Standards Met

National Health Education standards 4, 6, and 8

21st century student outcomes:

**Life and
Career Skills**

**Learning and
Innovation Skills**

**Information, Media,
and Technology Skills**

21st century interdisciplinary themes: Global awareness; financial, economic, business, and entrepreneurial literacy; civic literacy; health literacy; environmental literacy

Age Level

7+

Materials

Paper for flyers
Access to computer and printers
Markers or crayons
Recycling container (cardboard box or clean trash receptacle)
Plastic bags for collected cartridges

Recommended Procedures

1. This activity takes place over the course of nine weeks.
2. Identify a site or company that recycles ink cartridges.
3. Choose how the cartridges will be collected (door to door, at drop-off sites, or both).
4. Create and edit flyers. This can be done by students.
5. Decide when, where, and how to distribute flyers (e.g., neighborhoods, supermarkets, houses of worship, community centers).
6. Set a date for cartridge pickup. Choose two days in case of inclement weather, and instruct donors to leave cartridges on their doorsteps or porches for easy collection.
7. Volunteer collectors meet at the organization's central site (e.g., school, church, community center) to pick up their bags for collecting cartridges and to be assigned a collection area. They then go door to door in groups of two or three chaperoned by an adult if they are underage. Once their targeted areas have been canvassed, collectors return to the organization and turn in their cartridges.
8. The event director collects the cartridges, takes them to the recycling center, and collects the funds.

Event Preparation Time Line

Because this fundraiser is likely to be ongoing, we have set up the time line starting with the first activity going forward. All other activities have time lines that count backward.

Week 1

Young volunteers create the flyer soliciting donations of ink cartridges. They can make this on a computer or handwrite it. Flyers should provide a brief explanation as to who (e.g., Cub Scout group) is doing what (ink cartridge recycling) and why (e.g., to raise funds for a camping trip) and in what time frame (i.e., cartridges to be collected from doorsteps on [date] between the hours of [time] and [time]). Always provide an alternate means of contribution, such as monetary donations or donations of needed supplies.

Week 2

Young volunteers distribute flyers, and adult chaperones keep track of the addresses and businesses that have received flyers.

Weeks 3 through 8

This activity requires patience. We suggest that you allow six to eight weeks to elapse before collecting cartridges. You may want to distribute flyers to local businesses as well and direct them to a central drop-off site. E-mail blasts and automated phone messages can be sent a week before the collection date.

Week 9

Before sending them out to collect the cartridges, coach young volunteers in social skills such as shaking hands and expressing gratitude. After all the cartridges are collected, the director can bring or send them to the company chosen for reimbursement. Most companies give a check immediately. Find out ahead of time whether the company wants the cartridges to be separated by color, model, or make.

Postevent Processing and Evaluation

Discussion Questions for Students

What is the impact of recycling and reusing everyday materials?
What new computer skills did you learn from this activity?
How can community groups work together?
What is the appropriate salutation when greeting a neighbor?

Discussion Questions for Adults

What did you learn about mobilizing students and organizing their efforts?
Did you model socially responsible behavior?
Was the community supportive of this event?
How could this event have been more successful?

Sustainable Extension

This event can continue year round if community groups are aware of the event and your group has well-identified, clearly marked, and centrally located drop-off zones and collection points. Reminder notices can be sent out via e-mail blasts or signage in community areas.

Forms and Templates

Informational Flyer
Collection Data Sheet

INFORMATIONAL FLYER

[Name of organization]

[Town/city and state]

[Name of contact person and contact information]

Please support [Name of organization]; we are hoping to raise funds to [Use of funds; e.g., to offset the expense of our annual scouting badge ceremony camp-out at Blossom Lake].

We are collecting used printer ink cartridges of any type to recycle. Did you know that this activity not only raises funds but also benefits the environment and helps us protect the world we live in? Millions of ink cartridges are thrown away every day; it takes several cups of oil to produce new ink cartridges from scratch. Refunds for used cartridges can range from a few cents to as much as $3 depending on brand and ink color.

Six weeks from now, on [Two dates], we will come back to your home or office and collect used cartridges left out on your porch or doorstep. In the event of inclement weather, we will pick up these cartridges the following Saturday and Sunday. Feel free to contact [Name] at [Phone number] if you have any questions.

Thank you for supporting [Name of organization] and for protecting the environment.

You may also drop off additional cartridges at [Location] during the hours of [Hours], Monday through Friday. A receptacle is located in [Location].

From J. De Marzo, A. Gibbone, G. Letter, and C. Klein, 2012, *Healthy and sustainable fundraising activities* (Champaign, IL: Human Kinetics).

[Name of organization] Ink Cartridge Collection Drive

Name or business	Address	Flyer distributed	Cartridge pickup

From J. De Marzo, A. Gibbone, G. Letter, and C. Klein, 2012, *Healthy and sustainable fundraising activities* (Champaign, IL: Human Kinetics).

Hat Dayz

Activity Description

This activity raises low to moderate funds, while fostering community involvement without compromising the health and wellness of participants. Because hats are generally not allowed in schools and often at school-supported functions, nor are they generally a part of workplace attire, having the opportunity to wear a hat of any sort can be a novelty. This activity can be used to raise funds for your organization as well as for another nonprofit group or relief fund. Profits can be split between the earmarked organization and your own. This activity requires low-level knowledge, skills, and abilities on the part of volunteers and adult leaders. The title of the event can identify the secondary recipient of funds (e.g., Hats for Haitian Relief, Hats on for Clean Water).

Educational Objectives

Students will:

- Create advertisements on the computer (increasing their technological literacy) or by hand and disseminate information for the event, which will increase their involvement in your organization and in the larger community.
- Identify and help choose the organization for which funds will be raised.
- Recognize the value of philanthropic actions.
- Recognize the importance of civic engagement.
- Realize the dramatic impact their efforts can have on communities and people in need.
- Interact and communicate with others (neighbors and other students).
- Set and meet goals and demonstrate productivity and accountability.

Adults will:

- Mobilize students and organize their efforts with minimal hands-on time.
- Model socially responsible behavior as well as care and concern for neighbors and others.

The community will:

- Benefit from your organization's interest in promoting socially responsible behavior and community engagement.
- Experience increased cohesiveness from citizens working together.

Targeted Dimensions of Health

Social   **Mental**   **Emotional**   **Spiritual**

Standards Met

National Health Education standards 2, 4, 6, and 8
National Association for Sport and Physical Education standard 5
21st century student outcomes:

**Life and
Career Skills**

**Learning and
Innovation Skills**

**Information, Media,
and Technology Skills**

21st century interdisciplinary themes: Global awareness; financial, economic, business, and entrepreneurial literacy; civic literacy; health literacy; environmental literacy

Age Level

7+

Materials

Paper for flyers and posters
Access to the Internet and a printer
Access to local and community newspapers
Premade stickers, permission passes, or pins

Recommended Procedures

1. This activity is intended to take place on a single day. The intention is to make youngsters, supervisory adults, and community patrons aware of a health problem or need in their own community or afar. All participants pay for the privilege of wearing a hat in the workplace or at school.
2. Identify the date of the event.
3. Identify the earmarked organization if you are sharing the donations.
4. Identify donation sites such as the local library, a grocery store, or a strip mall.
5. Create flyers either electronically or by hand. This can be done by students.
6. Develop an automated message for delivery via a phone blast.
7. Distribute flyers via e-mail or by hand, and send an automatic phone message. Canvas the community to distribute flyers or post announcements at local sites around the community.
8. Establish a donation collection procedure. Adult supervisors or responsible youngsters can collect donations as participants enter the building on the designated day. Participants (can include staff and teachers at schools) make their donations and receive a sticker, pin, or certificate that they wear or display, along with or in lieu of a hat, throughout the day to identify them as participants.
9. You may choose to collect donations prior to the event. A few days before the event, supervised student volunteers can collect donations before or directly after the school day begins or ends. The same can be done a week prior to the event at centrally located community sites or at the office.
10. Young volunteers should be coached to use good communication skills when soliciting and collecting donations.

Event Preparation Time Line

One Month Prior to the Event

Young volunteers create a flyer or e-mail message advertising the hat dayz event. Flyers should provide a brief explanation of who (e.g., school or community organization) is doing what (collecting money in exchange for the privilege of wearing a hat to work or school) and why (e.g., to raise funds for a class trip or relief organization).

Three Weeks Prior to the Event

Flyer distribution, e-mail blasts, and phone calls via a school or work automated service should take place at this time. If you decide to include the whole community, you can advertise in local papers and post signs at local commercial sites to alert the public. Community events may require broader advertising and varied donation sites to create a successful fundraiser.

Two Weeks Prior to the Event

If your event is going to take place in a school or work environment, have participants purchase permission passes or premade stickers or labels announcing their commitment (e.g., I am wearing a hat for Haitian Relief for [designated amount]). People often donate more than the suggested amount, and some donate without participating.

One Week Prior to the Event

On the designated day of the hat dayz event, allow latecomers to participate and donate. If you are including the entire community, consider holding the event on a weekend when participants can wear their hats about town. You may want to synchronize your event with a time when your community comes together (e.g., Memorial Day parades, Friday night football games, homecoming, harvest festivals, Founders' Day). E-mail and automated phone messages can be resent the week of the event as a reminder.

Day of the Event

On the day of the event, be there early to set up and organize the collection site. If it will be at a school or workplace, the main entrance is the best place. Your group can set up a table or two to collect donations and hand out stickers to supporters that have not worn a hat but would like to participate.

After the Event

Collect all funds and deposit them immediately. Send a thank-you letter to the school principal who allowed the event or the CEO who allowed this event to take place at the worksite.

Postevent Processing and Evaluation

Discussion Questions for Students

What new skills did you learn in preparing for this event?
What impact has your participation in this event had on you?
What did you learn about the organization (e.g., Haitian Relief)?

Discussion Questions for Adults

What did you learn about mobilizing students, organizations, and communities?
Did you model socially responsible behavior?
Was the community, school, or workplace supportive of this event?
How might this event have been more successful?

Sustainable Extension

This event can be extended as a contest. The person with the most original or craziest hat can be awarded a prize or simply recognized in the school newsletter, the town newspaper, or an interoffice memo.

Forms and Templates

Sample Stickers and Labels
Invitation
Community Invitation

I'm supporting Hat Dayz!

Hatz for Haitian Relief! I'm a supporter!

From J. De Marzo, A. Gibbone, G. Letter, and C. Klein, 2012, *Healthy and sustainable fundraising activities* (Champaign, IL: Human Kinetics).

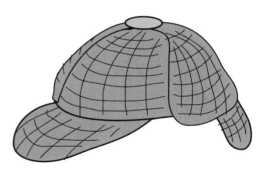

[Name organization]
Presents
Hat Dayz Event

Please join our community in raising funds for [Recipient organization] and [Name of organization].

On [Day and date], all students, faculty, and staff will be allowed to wear their favorite hat or cap to school! All participants must donate a pledge of $1.00 for the privilege of wearing a hat on that day. Student donations will be collected in homeroom on [Day and date], through [Day and date three days later]. Faculty and staff can pledge their donations to [Name of teacher] in [Room number].

Last-minute donations will be collected by [Name of collecting organization] at [Place] on Friday morning from 7 to 7:45 a.m.

If you would rather not wear a hat or cap but would like to donate, you will receive a hat dayz sticker!

We invite all community patrons, parents, and caregivers to support this event.

On behalf of [Name of organization], 25 percent of the proceeds will be donated to the [Recipient organization].

From J. De Marzo, A. Gibbone, G. Letter, and C. Klein, 2012, *Healthy and sustainable fundraising activities* (Champaign, IL: Human Kinetics).

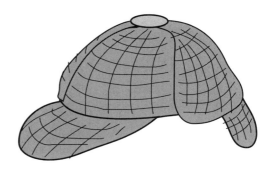

[Name organization]
Presents
Hat Dayz Event

Please join [Name of organization] in our fundraising event for [Recipient organization] and [Name of organization].

On [Day and date], all students, faculty, and staff will be allowed to wear their favorite hat or cap to school! All participants will donate a pledge of $1.00 for the privilege of wearing a hat on that day.

We invite all community patrons, parents, and caregivers to support this event. Donations will be collected by [Name of collecting group] in front of [Name of local business] and [Name of local business] in the [Name of shopping plaza or other site] on Saturday and Sunday, [Dates], from 12 noon to 4 p.m. Wear your favorite hat at Friday night's football game between [Name of team] and [Name of team] to show your support!

If you would rather not wear a hat or cap but would like to donate, you will receive a hat dayz sticker!

We will donate 25 percent of proceeds to [Recipient organization].

From J. De Marzo, A. Gibbone, G. Letter, and C. Klein, 2012, *Healthy and sustainable fundraising activities* (Champaign, IL: Human Kinetics).

Cell Phone Recycling

Activity Description

This is an ongoing cell phone recycling program that has the potential for raising substantial money while requiring very little setup and maintenance.

This activity will not only raise funds but also benefit the environment and teach young people their role in protecting the world they live in. It requires low-level knowledge, skills, and abilities on the part of young volunteers and adult leaders. This is a great beginner project and can be run concurrently with other fundraising projects.

Educational Objectives

Students will:

- Learn the impact of recycling and reusing everyday materials.
- Create their own announcements on the computer soliciting used cell phones and accessories from their families and neighbors.
- Interact and communicate with others (neighbors and other students).
- Set and meet goals, and demonstrate productivity and accountability.

Adults will:

- Mobilize students and organize their efforts with minimal hands-on time.
- Model socially responsible behavior as well as environmental literacy.

The community will:

- Benefit from your organization's interest in maintaining the integrity of the environment and of the larger community.
- Experience increased cohesiveness from citizens working together.

Targeted Dimensions of Health

Social

Mental

Environmental

Standards Met

National Health Education standards 4, 6, and 8
21st century student outcomes:

**Life and
Career Skills**

**Learning and
Innovation Skills**

**Information, Media,
and Technology Skills**

21st century interdisciplinary themes: Global awareness; financial, economic, business, and entrepreneurial literacy; civic literacy; health literacy; environmental literacy

Age Level

7+

Materials

Paper for flyers
Access to computer and printers
Markers or crayons
Recycling container (cardboard box or clean trash receptacle)
Plastic bags for collected cell phones

Recommended Procedures

1. This activity is intended to take place over the course of several weeks or even several months.
2. Identify a site or company that will recycle cell phones.
3. Choose how the cell phones will be collected (door to door, at drop-off sites, or both).
4. Create and edit flyers. Adult supervisors can direct young volunteers to create informational flyers either electronically or by hand, thus engaging children of all age groups and abilities.
5. Decide when, where, and how to distribute flyers (e.g., neighborhoods, supermarkets, houses of worship, community centers).
6. Set a date for cell phone pickup. Choose two days in case of inclement weather, and instruct donors to leave cartridges on their doorsteps or porches for easy collection.
7. Volunteer collectors meet at the organization's central site (e.g., school, church, community center) to pick up their bags for collecting cell phones and to be assigned a collection area. They then go door to door in groups of two or three chaperoned by an adult. Once their targeted areas have been canvassed, collectors return to the organization and turn in their cell phones.
8. If this is an ongoing activity, proper signage should be posted or flyers disseminated to direct donors to collection areas.
9. Once you have concluded the collection, the cell phones can be sent or brought to the chosen company. Numerous companies advertise on the Internet for used cell phones, and some even provide collection receptacles.

Event Preparation Time Line

One Month Prior to the Event

Young volunteers create the flyer soliciting donations of cell phones. They can make this on the computer or handwrite it. Flyers should provide a brief explanation as to who (e.g., Glenn Soccer Club) is doing what (cell phone recycling) and why (e.g., to raise funds for the spring tournament) and in what time frame (cell phones to be collected from doorsteps on [Date], between the hours of [Time] and [Time]). Always provide an alternate means of contribution such as monetary donations or donations of needed supplies. Determine which cell phone recycling company to use, so that you can be aware of any special requirements or packaging needs.

Three Weeks Prior to the Event

Volunteers distribute flyers, and adult chaperones keep track of the addresses and businesses that have received flyers.

Two Weeks Prior to the Event

Because most people have used cell phones lying around the house, a two-week lead time is sufficient. Flyers should be distributed two weeks before the collection day. Simultaneously, you should post flyers at local businesses as well and direct donations to central drop-off sites. If this activity is done within an organization, e-mail blasts and paper flyers can alert donors to (ongoing) centrally located collection sites. Adults should teach students appropriate social skills to use when collecting cell phones, such as shaking hands and expressing gratitude.

One Week Prior to the Event

Send e-mail blasts and electronic phone messages.

Day of the Event

At the collection site you might want to have signs or copies of the informational flyer available for any passerby that is interested in participating. Make sure your collection teams have bags or boxes to collect the phones. Have your volunteers be well versed in their salutations.

After the Event

Once the event is over, the phones can be counted up and separated if necessary as instructed by the recycling company. The sooner these collected phones are turned in to the recycling company, the sooner your efforts will be rewarded with profit for your organization.

Postevent Processing and Evaluation

Discussion Questions for Students

What is the impact of recycling and reusing everyday materials?
What new computer skills did you learn from this activity?
How can community groups work together?
What is the appropriate salutation when greeting a neighbor?

Discussion Questions for Adults

What did you learn about mobilizing students and organizing their efforts?
Did you model socially responsible behavior?
Was the community supportive of this event?
How could this event have been more successful?

Sustainable Extension

This event can continue year round if community groups are aware of the event and your group has well-identified, clearly marked, and centrally located drop-off sites and collection points. Reminder notices can be sent out via e-mail blasts or signage in community areas.

Forms and Templates

Informational Flyer

[Name of organization]
[Town/city and state]

[Name and contact information]

Please support [Name of organization]! We are hoping to raise funds to offset the expense of [Name of event].

We are collecting used cell phones of any type to recycle. Did you know that this activity not only raises funds but also benefits the environment and helps us protect the world we all live in? Many of you have had several cell phones. We also know that many of you have your old cell phones and their batteries lying around your homes. Those used phones can help [Name of organization] raise funds to offset the cost of [Name of event]. Recycled cell phones are often refurbished and sold in other countries, and the batteries are often replaced by new ones. Your old cell phone batteries must be disposed of properly so as not to pose a threat to our environment.

Two weeks from now, on Saturday, [Date], and Sunday, [Date], we will come back to your home or office to collect used cell phones (you may leave them out on your porch or stoop). In the event of inclement weather, we will attempt to pick up these cartridges the following Saturday, [Date]. If you prefer, we also accept monetary donations as well. Feel free to contact [Name] at [Phone number] if you have any questions.

Thank you for supporting [Name of organization] and for protecting the environment.

[Kids could sign their names here.]

You may also drop off used cell phones and their batteries at [Location] during the hours of [Hours], Monday through Friday. A receptacle is located at [Location].

From J. De Marzo, A. Gibbone, G. Letter, and C. Klein, 2012, *Healthy and sustainable fundraising activities* (Champaign, IL: Human Kinetics).

Cleanup Event

Activity Description

When selecting a fundraiser for your organization, you are sending a message to your participants as well as the community in which you will hold the event. At times it is prudent to get your organization behind a cause greater than your organization's financial needs. This earth-friendly event raises funds and sends a strong message about the environment at the same time. This is generally a one-day event in which you solicit pledges from the community. The pledges are tied to a specific goal (e.g., amount of garbage collected by weight, number of bags of leaves, length of road cleaned up measured in miles or kilometers). Your organization can choose a public park, the side of a road, a schoolyard, or even a residential property if the owners are game. You will be proud of what your volunteers' hard work accomplishes, and you will have plenty of proceeds to put to good use for your own cause.

Educational Objectives

Students will:

- Recognize the impact of their hard work on keeping the environment clean.
- Create their own announcements (flyers and e-mail blasts) on the computer and solicit pledges from their friends, families, and neighbors.
- Learn skills related to media and technology.
- Interact and communicate with others (neighbors and other students).
- Set and meet goals, and demonstrate productivity and accountability.

Adults will:

- Mobilize students and organize their efforts with minimal hands-on time.
- Model socially responsible behavior as well as environmental literacy.

The community will:

- Benefit from your organization's interest in the community as a whole, maintaining the integrity of the environment, and instilling in citizens a sense of social responsibility.
- Experience increased cohesiveness from citizens working together to create an event that is about more than just raising funds for a small sector of the greater community.

Targeted Dimensions of Health

Physical   **Social**   **Mental**   **Emotional**   **Spiritual**   **Environmental**

Standards Met

National Health Education standards 1, 2, 4, 6, and 8
National Association for Sport and Physical Education standards 5 and 6

21st century student outcomes:

**Life and
Career Skills**

**Learning and
Innovation Skills**

**Information, Media,
and Technology Skills**

21st century interdisciplinary themes: Global awareness; financial, economic, business, and entrepreneurial literacy; civic literacy; health literacy; environmental literacy

Age Level

Participants should be at least 10 years old for this activity because it requires some muscle strength and self-direction.

Materials

Paper for flyers
Access to computer and printers
Markers or crayons
Garbage bags
Garbage pails or dumpsters
Rakes, shovels, work gloves

Recommended Procedures

1. This activity occurs on a single day; the intention is to involve as many children, parents, and community members as possible.
2. Identify a cleanup event location.
3. Obtain permissions and permits.
4. Set the event date and a rain date.
5. Organize event committees of as small as two adults and two young volunteers.
6. Identify team captains for cleanup event crews.
7. Create flyers, e-mail blasts, and social networking messages to get the word out. Flyers can be handmade or done on the computer by young volunteers. Adults and older student volunteers can also have a hand in creating these, too.
8. Arrange for picking up garbage or leaves.
9. Get the community sanitation department involved to determine how much garbage or leaves were collected and to help with pickup and disposal.
10. Solicit pledges prior to the event. For example, community members can pledge a penny for every pound or kilogram of garbage collected, or for every bag of garbage or leaves collected.

Event Preparation Time Line

Three Months Prior to the Event

Setting a Date

You might find that having the cleanup event on the same day as another event is effective (e.g., after a rubber duck race or stop, drop, and roll fire safety event). Stacking two events at one time maximizes your efforts and may negate the necessity for holding another event later in the year.

Organizing Event Committees

Cleanup events are often done in teams. You might consider identifying coaches to oversee the teams and be in contact with team captains. Team captains are people willing to be responsible for communicating with coaches, collecting solicited funds, and making sure other team members are prepared and present on the day of the cleanup event.

Several managers may be required depending on how big an area you intend to clean up and how many young volunteers need to be supervised. The main role of the managers is to organize the logistics of the day. They assign groups to specific areas in the cleanup event zone and make sure teams have the proper tools and garbage bags. Managers must also be on the lookout for safety issues (hydration, protection from sun) and must keep track of all team members. As far as tools go, many municipalities provide garbage bags and receptacles and also loan rakes, brooms, and shovels if you are cleaning up their parks.

Creating a Publicity Committee

Depending on the size of your event, you may need more than one person or a team for publishing flyers, sending out e-mail blasts, posting on your website, sending out ads to local papers, making announcements at functions, and sending invitations (or e-vites) to members.

Nominating a Banker or Cashier

The banker, or cashier, is responsible for collecting money and determining which methods of payment will be accepted (i.e., credit cards, checks). If you decide to accept credit cards, you will need to arrange a method for processing the payments. Participants are paid by people who have pledged prior to the event based on how much garbage or how many bags of leaves they collect.

Two Months Prior to the Event

Send out a letter (via regular mail, e-mail, or both) or post a notice on your website asking for participation and prize donations. Be sure to also write to community businesses for prize donations for rubber duck race winners. A well-written letter along with a contribution form can help you bring in items for your event (see Forms and Templates). Here are a number of ways to solicit pledges and donations:

Hand out and post flyers around the community (see Forms and Templates).
Posts on social networking sites.
Send e-mails to e-mail lists.
Send press releases (see Forms and Templates).
Send letters to members.
Make announcements at meetings.
Send invitations (see Forms and Templates).
Create and distribute pledge sheets (see Forms and Templates).

Invite groups from around the community (e.g., soccer teams, baseball teams, church groups) to participate in groups of four or five. You can use incentives such as free movie passes, free skate passes to the local roller or ice rink, or a homework pass for the team that collects the most donations, trash, or leaves. There is never too much help. Young children who can't organize themselves can be mixed into other groups, thereby providing a new venue for socialization.

One Month Prior to the Event

Talk it up! The more noise you make about your event, the more people you will attract. At this point you should have volunteers signed up either as teams or individually. Place individual participants in teams, and post these groupings the morning of the event. Pledge sheets and donations should be turned in to the banker, or cashier.

It is a good idea to send out e-mail blasts or to display posters to tell the public how much money was pledged and how near or far you are from your goal.

At this time, managers should secure all the tools and supplies needed for ensuring a smooth event (e.g., rakes, garbage bags, dumpsters, shovels, work gloves). Managers should also consider setting up a water station and a first aid table.

Day of the Event

Arrive early! Set up water stations and first aid tables, and set out tools, garbage bags, and receptacles. Post teams and determine the areas they will be responsible for cleaning. During the event make sure everyone is hydrated and that a shady spot is available for those in need. Announce periodically how much time is left, and determine a site where participants can deposit their tools and unused garbage bags.

Have a participant registry to gather e-mail addresses or home addresses from all attendees so you can send out thank-you notes and announcements for next year's event.

Once the event has concluded, announce the amount of trash and donations collected. The community sanitation department should be able to estimate how much trash was collected; in some communities, they may actually weigh the materials at truck weigh stations.

Within one month following the event, send letters or electronic thank-you notes to donors and participants (see Forms and Templates).

Postevent Processing and Evaluation

Discussion Questions for Students

What is the impact of a clean or polluted environment?
What new computer skills did you learn from this activity?
How can community groups work together?
What is an appropriate salutation when greeting a neighbor?

Discussion Questions for Adults

What did you learn about mobilizing students and organizing their efforts?
Did you model socially responsible behavior?
Was the community supportive of this event?
How could this event have been more successful?

Sustainable Extension

This event can be performed as a seasonal kick-off event. It might also be used as an alternative spring break activity. It is great for times when students and community members are likely to be outside or are out of school and have more time to spare.

Forms and Templates

Informational Flyer
Sample Press Release

Cleanup Event

Please join [Name of organization] on [Date]

9 a.m. to 12 p.m. at [Location]

Volunteers are needed to participate in this [Name of cleanup event]. Pledge your support to youth volunteers! Our goal is to collect a ton of garbage. Pledges range from a penny to a nickel per pound of trash collected from the site. All proceeds go to [Recipient organization].

Please contact [Name] at [Phone number] to donate items for this event. Our success depends on your generosity!

From J. De Marzo, A. Gibbone, G. Letter, and C. Klein, 2012, *Healthy and sustainable fundraising activities* (Champaign, IL: Human Kinetics).

For Immediate Release

CONTACT: [Name] at [Phone number]

[Town/city and state]—[Name of organization] of [Name of township] will hold a cleanup event on [Date] at [Location]. All proceeds will be donated to [Recipient organization], which [Describe the work of the recipient organization].

   This cleanup event raised over [Amount raised] last year for [Work of recipient organization] and hopes to increase that amount this year.

   The funds will be used to [Describe the work of the recipient organization]. We are excited to be able to bring back some of the programming that was cut due to budget constraints.

   [Name of organization] is currently soliciting donations for the cleanup event. If you would like to contribute supplies or monetary donations or attend the event, please contact [Name] at [Phone number] or check out our website at [Website address].

From J. De Marzo, A. Gibbone, G. Letter, and C. Klein, 2012, *Healthy and sustainable fundraising activities* (Champaign, IL: Human Kinetics).

Scrip Event

Activity Description

Scrip fundraising offers nonprofit organizations the opportunities to raise funds without asking people to spend a penny more than they already do. Scrip enables people to help your fundraising efforts while they make their normal purchases. Your organization takes orders for gift certificates or gift cards from supporters and buys them at a discount from local or national merchants. Scrip is then used just like cash in their stores or on their websites.

When scrip certificates are purchased in advance of shopping, your organization earns a percentage of every purchase eventually made with scrip. These local and national merchants contribute anywhere from 2 to 25 percent of everything purchased with scrip by your supporters. Over time, these percentages can add up to a considerable amount. Your organization may choose to buy scrip directly from retailers or through a scrip service that buys for you. This fundraiser can be done in addition to other fundraisers. It can also be done year round with a scrip coordinator and handled via your website or take-home order forms.

Educational Objectives

Students will:

- Improve their financial, economic, and entrepreneurial literacy.
- Develop a greater sense of their saving and spending power and recognize how planning ahead can save considerable money.
- Improve their civic and environmental literacy.
- Increase their innovation skills by focusing on creativity, communication, and collaboration.

Adults will:

- Help students develop social skills as well as flexibility, self-direction, team building, productivity, accountability, and leadership.

The community will:

- Benefit from young people learning the skills necessary to be productive citizens in today's challenging world.
- Benefit from citizens modeling prosocial and socially responsible civic behavior to youngsters.
- Be able to support this fundraiser at no additional cost. Consumers will spend money on necessary items anyway, such as groceries, gasoline, and retail items. By purchasing scrip they will be supporting the organization and getting their everyday needs satisfied.

Targeted Dimensions of Health

Social

Mental

Spiritual

Emotional

Environmental

Standards Met

National Health Education standards 4 and 8
21st century student outcomes:

**Life and
Career Skills**

**Learning and
Innovation Skills**

**Information, Media,
and Technology Skills**

21st century interdisciplinary themes: Global awareness; financial, economic, business, and entrepreneurial literacy; civic literacy; environmental literacy

Age Level

Volunteers must be at least 12 years old. Student participation is limited.

Materials

Paper for flyers and posters
Access to the Internet for e-mail blasts and social networking posts
Access to local and community newspapers

Recommended Procedures

Scrip fundraising is novel to many people; however, purchasing gift cards and gift certificates is not. To promote this event well, you need to explain how prepurchasing scrip saves money. You also need to identify the services or items you are offering. Gas companies and supermarket chains are seeing a rise in prepurchased cards as a result of rising gas and food prices. Assessing the needs of your community in terms of geographic locale will help you identify sought-after scrip (e.g., snow removal, leaf pickup, car washes).

Event Preparation Time Line

Three Months Prior to the Event

Setting a Date and Getting Started

First, make sure to set a date. Then select one or two scrip coordinators to oversee the ordering and distribution process. Recruit adult volunteers to help with launching, promoting, and advertising your scrip event. Decide whether you will order scrip directly from retailers or use a scrip company. If you decide to order directly from retailers, you will have to negotiate with several retailers individually. If you use a scrip company, you can order a variety of retailer scrip at one time because these companies represent a number of retailers.

Students may be involved if scrip is to be sold to family members, friends, and neighbors. Families are often the most generous in fundraising activities, so students may be able to raise funds within their immediate and extended families. If you want to cast a wider net and fundraise beyond students' immediate families, you could encourage them to extend their reach to neighbors, coaches, and parents' coworkers. Students can also help with advertising, making and distributing flyers and e-flyers, and posting to social networks.

Nominating a Banker or Cashier

A banker, or cashier, is responsible for collecting money and determining which methods of payment will be accepted (i.e., credit cards, checks) and has cash on hand for change (if you are doing a table event). If you decide to accept credit cards, you will need to arrange a method for processing payments.

Opening a Separate Checking Account

A separate checking account for your scrip fundraiser is helpful for both balancing your books and ensuring security.

Determining your fundraising goals will help supporters identify with the program. At this point you also need to determine your ordering and distribution process. You can create a custom order form if ordering directly from retailers. If you are using a company, you can order directly from the company, which can then send gift cards (scrip) directly to supporters or to you for distribution. You also need to decide whether you will carry an inventory of scrip or order it as necessary. If supporters will be collecting their scrip from you, you will need to determine where and when distribution will take place.

Two Months Prior to the Event

To promote your scrip fundraiser, send a letter (via regular mail, e-mail, or both) or post a request for contributions to your website. Be sure to send letters requesting support to other community organizations (see Forms and Templates). Here are a number of ways you can solicit orders for scrip donations:

Hand out and post flyers around the community (see Forms and Templates).
Post to social networking sites.
Send e-mails to e-mail lists.
Send letters to members and supporters.
Make announcements at meetings.
Schedule an informational meeting (e.g., What is scrip?).

You may want to offer additional incentives (free scrip, raffles) to supporters who sell the most script; this can be made into a competition among classes, teams, or troops. Remind business owners to use scrip to purchase business-related supplies. Also, remember to purchase all school and church supplies or other items using scrip!

One Month Prior to the Event

Start selling scrip! If student volunteers are selling to family, friends, and neighbors, periodically update them on their progress. Communicating with your volunteers at every opportunity keeps them updated on the program's progress and may contribute to their totals. Sell scrip at sporting events and after-school activities. Create a monthly newsletter. Run ads in your church bulletin or newsletter. Continue to send e-mail blasts to supporters, and use social networking sites to further develop your supporter base.

Concluding the Scrip Event

Depending on how you conducted your scrip event, you may or may not establish a firm concluding date. If your fundraiser is to go on for a few months, periodic updates are really important. If you decide on an end date, publicize it and urge late supporters to contribute. You may want to offer special incentives (e.g., anyone who purchases $200 in scrip by December 15 receives a $5 coupon for Joe's Pizza).

Once the event has concluded, announce totals and incentive winners. Within one month following the event, if feasible, send letters or electronic thank-you notes to donors and community supporters (see Forms and Templates).

Hold a wrap-up meeting with the committees to discuss what worked well and what should be changed for the next event. Keep a record of donors for your next event.

Postevent Processing and Evaluation

Discussion Questions for Students

How might prepurchasing gift and service cards save families money?
Can prepurchasing scrip help families stay within a budget?
What new computer skills did you learn from this activity?
How can community groups work together?
What have you learned about greeting neighbors?

Discussion Questions for Adults

What advertisement techniques seemed to work best?
Is having a rolling fundraiser more or less profitable than one that has a start and end date?
Was the community supportive of this event?
How could this event have been more successful?

Sustainable Extension

There are several ways to turn your scrip event into an even larger moneymaker. To draw an even bigger crowd, cross-promote with other groups. Bigger events often add live auctions, silent auctions, raffles, sponsorships, and entertainment from a band or DJ, all of which can help you raise considerably more funds for your group.

Forms and Templates

Informational Flyer
Informational Letter
Sample Introductory Letter
Thank-you Letter to Scrip Purchaser

What Is Scrip?

Scrip is a term that means "substitute money." When you purchase scrip, you're purchasing negotiable gift certificates and prepaid cards that are used just like cash. You can use scrip to purchase everyday expenses such as food, clothing, and other essentials, and with every purchase, you earn revenue for our organization.

How Scrip Generates Revenue

Scrip can be purchased from retailers with cash up front. There are also scrip companies that act on behalf of churches, schools, and other nonprofit organizations to purchase large amounts of scrip from grocery stores, department stores, and other retailers. Because the scrip is purchased with cash up front, the participating retailers offer substantial discounts. Our organization will buy the scrip from retailers directly at a discount and resell the certificates to families like yours for full face value. The discount—from 2 to 25 percent or more—is our organization's revenue.

Scrip Is "Shopping Cart Fundraising"

Scrip is a popular fundraiser because no selling is required. Organization members produce revenue by making regular household purchases they would make anyway. Groceries, clothing, toys, gifts, and even gasoline can be purchased with scrip.

Find Out More

Ask your scrip coordinator, listed below, for the latest participating retailer list. Then put your shopping dollars to work for our organization!

[Name of organization]
[Name of contact person]
[Phone number and e-mail address of contact person]

From J. De Marzo, A. Gibbone, G. Letter, and C. Klein, 2012, *Healthy and sustainable fundraising activities* (Champaign, IL: Human Kinetics).

Major Retailers Want to Give Our School Money!

Dear [Name of organization] parent [or member],

We're pleased to share some exciting news about a new fundraising program for [Name of organization]. It's called scrip, and it's the fundraising program that works while you shop.

Scrip is simply a word that means "substitute money"—in other words, gift certificates from national and local retailers. They are the same gift certificates that you buy at the store. Many popular retailers participate in our scrip program including J.C. Penney, The Gap, Shell, Pizza Hut, Red Lobster, and many others.

You're probably asking yourself how these stores help us raise money. It's simple: participating retailers agree to sell gift certificates to our organization at a discount. Member families such as yours buy the certificates for full face value, they redeem them for full face value, and [Name of organization] keeps the difference as revenue. Scrip is exciting, because everybody wins:

- The retailer gets cash up front and repeat business.
- You get a powerful fundraising alternative that involves no selling.
- [Name of organization] gets a regular source of revenue.

The beauty of scrip is that you put your regular household shopping dollars to work. You earn money for [Name of organization] without spending a single additional penny. Just spend your regular shopping dollars with scrip at the stores that participate in the scrip program! And scrip can be used for just about any household purchase including food, clothing, entertainment, gasoline, and even dining out.

We will be holding a series of brief informational meetings about our new scrip program, and we urge you to attend. We will go over all the facts about scrip, provide enrollment forms, and answer your questions.

[Name of organization] Scrip Informational Meeting
[Date and time]
[Location]

The [Name of organization] scrip program promises to be a simple and effective fundraising program. Thanks for your support, and we'll see you at one of our meetings!

Sincerely,

[Name]
Scrip program spokesperson
[Phone number]
[E-mail address]

From J. De Marzo, A. Gibbone, G. Letter, and C. Klein, 2012, *Healthy and sustainable fundraising activities* (Champaign, IL: Human Kinetics).

Scrip Fundraising Has Arrived!

A new and exciting fundraising program called scrip is available at [Name of organization]. Now you can raise money without buying unwanted items, selling door to door, polluting the earth, or increasing your waistline. Supporting our programs has never been easier!

How It Works

Scrip refers to gift certificates or gift cards. [Name of organization] is able to purchase gift cards from hundreds of retailers nationwide at a discount, which you can then buy at face value. The difference is our profit. These are the same gift cards that you would purchase if you went to the retailer directly. By purchasing these gift cards before you shop for your everyday items—such as groceries, gas, clothes, and restaurant meals—you donate money to [Name of organization] without having to spend a penny extra. It's just that simple.

Help Us Reach Our Goal

Our goals this year are twofold: [State goals]. With scrip, our goal is to raise [Amount] in the next year. With an average profit return of 5 percent, if your family buys $400 worth of gift cards per month, you would raise $240 for our programs. If just 100 families do this, we will meet our goal.

How to Participate

Simply return the attached order form with your check to [Location] by [Day and time]. You will receive a new order form each week. You may pick up your order on [Day] at [Location].

We encourage you to take advantage of the wonderful benefits offered by this ongoing fundraiser. If you have questions, please contact [Name] at [Phone number]. Help us exceed our goals, and thank you in advance for your support!

Sincerely,

[Name]

THANK-YOU LETTER TO SCRIP PURCHASER

[Date]

[Name]
[Company or affiliation]
[Address]

Dear [Name],

Thank you for your generous support by purchasing scrip. Your purchase will benefit the [Recipient organization].

Thanks to you and other donors like you, we were able to raise over [Amount] for [Recipient organization]. The beauty of scrip is that you put your regular household shopping dollars to work. You earn money for our program without spending a single additional penny.

We are planning to hold this fundraiser event again next [Month] and will again try to increase the number of scrip purchased to raise funds for [Recipient organization]. I hope we can count on your support for our next event.

Thank you again for your generosity.

Sincerely,

[Name]
[Year] Event Chair

From J. De Marzo, A. Gibbone, G. Letter, and C. Klein, 2012, *Healthy and sustainable fundraising activities* (Champaign, IL: Human Kinetics).

Stop, Drop, and Roll Fire Safety Event

Activity Description

This activity raises low to moderate funds while contributing to the health and wellness of the community and the participants, particularly in the area of fire safety. In addition to raising funds for your organization, this activity educates participants and volunteers about the risk of fire in the home while providing parents, children, and caregivers life-saving skills. It requires a low level of knowledge, skills, and abilities from young volunteers, but a moderate level of organizational skills from adult volunteers. It is straightforward and easy to extend and modify.

Educational Objectives

Students will:

- Understand the value of fire safety awareness and preparedness.
- Create their own announcement on the computer or by hand to advertise the community event.
- Interact and communicate with others (neighbors and other students).
- Set and meet goals, and demonstrate productivity and accountability.
- Identify the role of community helpers and professionals.
- Understand their civic responsibility.

Adults will:

- Mobilize students and organize their efforts with moderate hands-on time.
- Model socially responsible behavior and demonstrate civic literacy.

The community will:

- Benefit from your organization's interest in fostering both health and safety literacy while supporting civic responsibility within the community.
- Experience increased cohesiveness from citizens working together.

The following are additional objectives that are likely to be met with this activity. Participants will have a better understanding of the dangers of smoke. They will:

- Recognize that smoke is a poison and that if they breathe it in, they will choke.
- Understand that hearing is the only active sense when they are sleeping.
- Understand that a smoke detector is the best fire warning.
- Recognize the sound of a smoke detector and understand that when they hear one, they must get out and stay out.

Participants will learn about exits. They will:

- Understand the importance of knowing the exits from a room or building, whether marked or not.

- Understand the need to escape from a burning building.

Participants will understand why it is best to crawl under smoke. They will:

- Learn that smoke is lighter than air and fills a room from the top down.
- Recognize the importance of crawling anytime there is smoke in a room.
- Practice the crawl-under-smoke procedure.

Participants will be able to demonstrate the stop, drop, and roll technique if their clothes, bodies, or hair ever catch fire. They will:

- Understand the importance of not walking or running around if their clothes are on fire (i.e., that they must stop).
- Learn that the best thing to do when they are on fire is to drop to the ground.
- Practice rolling on the ground to extinguish any flames or embers on their clothes or bodies.

Targeted Dimensions of Health

Physical   **Social**   **Mental**   **Emotional**   **Spiritual**   **Environmental**

Standards Met

National Health Education standards 1, 4, 5, 7, and 8
National Association for Sport and Physical Education standards 1, 2, 5, and 6
21st century student outcomes:

**Life and
Career Skills**   **Learning and
Innovation Skills**   **Information, Media,
and Technology Skills**

21st century interdisciplinary themes: Civic literacy; health literacy; environmental literacy

Age Level

Student volunteers must be at least 10 years old. Community participants can be preschool age and older.

Materials

Paper for flyers
Access to computers
Golf balls
Tables
Fire safety information (free online)
Local fire department volunteers and demonstrative devices and equipment

Recommended Procedures

This activity is intended to take place on a single day as a fire safety event. It can also be done in conjunction with a community fair or school or community function.

The stop, drop, and roll drill is taught to nearly every preschool child in the United States. Children are taught that if their clothes or bodies are on fire, they must *stop* immediately (running fans the flames). They must then *drop* to the ground immediately and *roll* around to extinguish the flames.

After demonstrating the stop, drop, and roll technique, each participant receives a numbered golf ball and stands and rolls it toward a target. All participants can do this at once or a few at a time. The target may be either a hole in the ground or a painted circle in the middle of a field or gymnasium. Another option is to have participants drop their golf balls into a net. The net is suspended from the cherry picker on a fire truck, which is positioned above a bull's eye painted on a field. The balls are released, and the one that lands closest to the target or in the hole is the winner of the competition. If there is a tie, combine the prize (e.g., tickets to events) and split it between the two winners. Each participant pays for the golf ball and the opportunity to stop, drop, and roll. They can purchase several golf balls.

Both versions of this competition (rolling balls individually or dropping them all from a net) have great spectator appeal.

You can have several fundraisers going at one time. Different groups can run different activities, and you can also invite other organizations to cohost the event. Again, running more than one activity at the same time can increase your fundraising potential. You might have a simple 50/50 raffle at the event or a raffle for prizes other than money. You can also sell refreshments and yield a profit there as well. This technique is called stacking.

Event Preparation Time Line

Three Months Prior to the Event

Setting a Date

You may find that having this event on the same day as another event is effective (e.g., Back to School Night, PTA elections). You can also run it in conjunction with another activity to double your fundraising efforts.

Organizing an Event or Raffle Committee

Because a successful raffle requires a lot of work, consider dividing the committee into two groups: one to focus on procuring raffle items and the other to focus on the logistics of the raffle. We recommend the following structure for a stop, drop, and roll committee.

Raffle Chair and Co-Chair

The primary qualifications for the chair are a willingness to serve in this capacity and the ability to lead others. The chair assembles and leads the committee in setting ambitious and realistic goals for the event. Co-chairs can share responsibilities or one can ultimately lead while the other supports the first; this depends on the dynamics of the volunteers.

Procurement Team

The procurement team solicits contributions (for prizes or necessary materials) to the event. These people must have the time and willingness to contact members or potential donors by phone or in person for donations. They need to be friendly and persuasive. This team can be divided into those who solicit from members and those who solicit within the community at large.

Arrangements Team

Depending on the size of your event, you may need more than one person or a team for each of the following areas.

Publicity

The publicity team publishes flyers, sends out e-mail blasts, sets up posts on websites, sends out ads to local papers, makes announcements at organization functions, and sends invitations (and e-vites) to members.

Setup

The setup team is responsible for coordinating with the facility where the event will take place. This includes setting up tables, displaying items, posting signs, and cleaning up.

Banking

The banker, or cashier, is responsible for totaling up each participant's bill and collecting money. The banker also determines which methods of payment will be accepted (i.e., credit cards, checks) and makes sure to have cash on hand for making change. If you decide to accept credit cards, you will need to arrange a method for processing payments.

Contacting Your Local Fire Department

Many fire departments have information for parents, children, and residents on fire prevention. Many are volunteer organizations and are chartered to engage in community service. Your local fire department may be willing to conduct a presentation on smoke detectors: where to get them and how to make sure they are working. Some provide free or low-cost smoke detectors to community residents. Most fires in which children have died were in homes that did not have working smoke detectors. Fire departments may also give demonstrations on crawling, explaining that smoke is lighter than air and therefore fills a room from the top down. Firefighters may even demonstrate the crawl-under-smoke procedure.

Here is important information from fire departments:

- Leave the firefighting to the professionals. If you cannot put out a contained fire (i.e., one that is very small and has not started to spread) with a fire extinguisher in less than 20 seconds, *leave the building*.

- Do not try to use a fire extinguisher for the first time when there is an actual fire. Your local fire department may be willing to show you how to properly use a fire extinguisher. Get instructions and practice using it before you actually have to. At a moment's notice, it won't be easy to just read the instructions and use it correctly.

- Never assume that you have enough time. It takes only a few seconds to a few minutes before flames can spread through an entire home. Leave a burning home as quickly as possible.

- The heat of a fire is more deadly than the flames. The heat of a fire can rise to 600 degrees Fahrenheit (315 °C). Such heat is deadly and can melt clothes to the skin. Don't think that if you don't see flames you are safe.

- Once a flame starts, thick, black smoke quickly follows. The dark smoke prevents you from seeing—and breathing.

- Smoke and the toxic gases and fumes from fire are more deadly than the flames. Breathing becomes difficult. Smoke inhalation is the major cause of injury in a fire.

If you do not have an active fire department that is willing to demonstrate or discuss these issues, you can create your own demonstrations and information booths. Organizations have created mock houses (mazes) out of cardboard and conducted fire drills; demonstrated the crawl; and explained how to identify exits, position smoke detectors, establish a central meeting spot after escaping a fire, and dialing the emergency number (911 in the United States). Websites on fire safety and prevention procedures also offer a lot of useful information. Many provide lesson plans and directions for drawing up an escape plan, as well as information on fire safety recalls of children's products, publications, and educational resources.

U.S. Fire Administration for Kids: www.usfa.fema.gov/kids/flash.shtm

U.S. Fire Administration, Fire Safety Campaign for Babies and Toddlers: www. usfa.fema. gov/campaigns/usfaparents/

FEMA (Federal Emergency Management Administration) for Kids and Resources for Parents and Teachers: www.ready.gov/kids

Two Months Prior to the Event

Send out a letter (by regular mail, e-mail blast, or both) and post to your website asking members and supporters for contributions. You can also send a letter or e-mail to community businesses asking for donations. A well-written letter along with a donation form can help you bring in items for your event (see Forms and Templates). Here are a number of ways to solicit donations for raffle items:

Hand out and post flyers around the community.
Post on social networking sites.
Send e-mails to e-mail lists.
Send press releases (see Forms and Templates).
Send letters to members.
Make announcements at meetings.
Send invitations (see Forms and Templates).

Procuring Raffle Items

The best ways to procure items is to contact the members of your organization; you can also approach area businesses.

- Send out a letter (see Forms and Templates) to each of your members soliciting donations. Be sure to mention that the money raised will benefit your organization. You can suggest items to contribute as well as monetary donations to be used to purchase items such as gift baskets, sporting equipment, holiday items, stationery and gift wrap, toys, electronics, books, and autographed memorabilia.

- Two to four weeks after sending the letter, phone members who have not responded and ask for donations.

- Complete a donation form (see Forms and Templates) for each item that is donated, and give it to the setup team. The setup team will keep track of items, establish what starting bids will be or if the item will be part of the raffle, and so on. All items should be logged; when sending out thank-you letters, you can refer to the specific item and donor. Make sure each form is filled out completely. The street address and e-mail address are important so you can send a thank-you following the event. Arrange to pick up the items prior to the day of the event to be sure they make it.

Talk it up! The more noise you make about your event, the more people you will attract. Send out invitations in as many forms as you can.

Flyers and Advertisements

- Student-created flyers can be posted either electronically or by hand. They should explain briefly who (your organization) is doing what (donate a dollar for the chance to stop, drop, and roll [a golf ball] for fire safety event) and why (e.g., to raise funds for a class trip or new books or art supplies). Identify the time, date, and location at which contributions will be collected. If you are collecting donations within the community, check to see whether permission is required. Always provide an alternate means of contribution such as monetary donations or donations of needed supplies.

- Develop an automated message to send via phone blast to the community.

- Distribute flyers within your organization or via e-mail or phone message. Canvas the community to distribute flyers or post announcement at local sites around the community.

- Identify your raffle or donation procedure. For example, have adult supervisors or responsible students collect donations as students enter the school building on the designated day. Each donor receives a numbered raffle ticket.

- The most attractive raffle prizes are big cash prizes for first-place winners followed by smaller cash prizes for lower-level winners.

- You can also add smaller noncash prizes that have been donated, so that everyone entered has a larger chance of winning something.

- You can offer prize money of up to 50 percent of raffle ticket sales and still raise a substantial sum. Half of the available prize money should be committed to the grand prize, and the balance should be used in declining amounts as you set the number of prizes (e.g., $500 for first prize, $250 for second prize, $150 for third prize, and so on).

One Month Prior to the Event

- Determine which methods of payment you will accept. The more methods you offer, the easier it is for people to buy. Arrange to have cash on hand to make change.

- Arrange for a credit card processing machine if you will be accepting credit cards.

- Coordinate volunteers to declare winning golf balls.

- Start selling raffle tickets. You may be surprised at how many tickets you can sell before the event. You can sell in blocks of 10, 20, or even 100 chances. Each numbered ticket matches a numbered golf ball in the drop. Larger groups can easily sell several thousand raffle tickets. You can request or mandate that each member of the organization or student volunteer sell a specified number of tickets.

Day of the Event

Arrive early! Set up tables, items, the golf ball drop zone, and a cashier's table. During the event be mindful of time constraints; announce periodically how much time is left for participation and purchasing raffle tickets. Encourage participants to donate in other ways (e.g., monetary donations). Have a participant registry to obtain e-mail addresses or home addresses from all attendees so you can send out thank-you notes and announcements for next year's event.

Once the event has concluded, announce the winners, collect donations, and distribute prizes.

After the Event

Deposit the funds immediately. Send thank-you letters to everyone who contributed a prize to the event and to all community sponsors and organizations that assisted in the event. Hold a wrap-up meeting with the event committees to discuss what worked well and what should be changed for the next event. Also, keep a record of donors for your next event.

Postevent Processing and Evaluation

Discussion Questions for Students

Why is it important to know fire safety?
Do you think this activity had an impact on the community?
What new skills did you learn from this activity?

Discussion Questions for Adults

What did you learn about mobilizing students and organizing their efforts?
What were some of the pitfalls you encountered in organizing community helpers?
Was the community supportive of this event?
How could this event have been more successful?

Sustainable Extension

There are several ways to turn your stop, drop, and roll event into an even larger moneymaker. One way is to sell food and drinks. Another is to add other family-oriented fundraising activities such as inflatable bouncers, a temporary tattoo booth, a ball-toss game, or a dunking tank.

To draw an even bigger crowd, cross-promote with other groups. Bigger events often add live auctions, silent auctions, sponsorships, and entertainment from a band or DJ, all of which can raise considerably more funds for your group.

Forms and Templates

Invitation
Sample Press Release
Sample Newsletter Article
Sample Procurement Letter
Donation Form
Thank-You Letter to Donor
Thank-You Letter to Community Organizations

Stop, Drop, and Roll Fire Safety Event

Please join [Name of organization] on [Date]

9 a.m. to 12 p.m. at [Location]

All Proceeds go to [Recipient organization].

Winners of the event will receive prizes that include [List prizes; e.g., a 70-inch plasma TV, MP3 players, a Blu-ray disc player, dinner for two, a weekend getaway package].

[Your local fire department] will be on site to demonstrate fire safety procedures for you and your family.

Please contact [Name] at [Phone number] to donate prize items for this event. Our success depends on your generosity!

For Immediate Release

CONTACT: [Name] at [Phone number]

[Name of organization] to Hold Stop, Drop, and Roll Fire Safety Event

[Town, State]—[Name of organization] will hold its third annual stop, drop, and roll fire safety event on [Date] at [Location]. All proceeds from the event will be donated to [Recipient organization] that [Brief description of the work of the recipient organization].

Stop, drop, and roll raised over $1,100 last year for [Recipient organization] and we hope to increase that amount this year.

Funds are used to [Work of recipient organization]. We are excited to be able to give back some of the programming that was cut as a result of budget constraints.

[Name of organization] is currently soliciting donations of prizes for the stop, drop, and roll fire safety event. If you would like to contribute or attend the event, please contact [Name], chair, at [Phone number].

From J. De Marzo, A. Gibbone, G. Letter, and C. Klein, 2012, *Healthy and sustainable fundraising activities* (Champaign, IL: Human Kinetics).

It's Fire Safety Month!

Mark your calendar and make plans to attend the [Name of organization] third annual stop, drop, and roll fire safety event to be held on [Date] during [Another event, or add location].

This is your chance to get outside and support [Work of the recipient organization]. All proceeds from stop, drop, and roll will go to [Recipient organization]. Last year we raised over [Amount], and we hope to raise more this year. Plan to attend; bring a friend; and stop, drop, and roll a few golf balls while learning fire safety procedures.

Also, we are still collecting prize items for winners. If you or your company would like to contribute to this worthwhile event, please contact [Name], chair, by calling [Phone number].

From J. De Marzo, A. Gibbone, G. Letter, and C. Klein, 2012, *Healthy and sustainable fundraising activities* (Champaign, IL: Human Kinetics).

[Date]

[Name]
[Address]

Dear [Name],

I would like to invite you to participate in a very special event. For the third year in a row, [Name of organization] will be holding a stop, drop, and roll fire safety event at [Location], on [Date], to benefit [Recipient organization], and we need your help to make it a success.

All proceeds from stop, drop, and roll will be donated to [Recipient organization], a not-for-profit organization that [Work of recipient organization].

The work of [Recipient organization] is supported by tax deductible contributions made by individuals, companies, and organizations.

Here's how you can help:

1. Please consider contributing an item to the stop, drop, and roll fire safety event. The item can be donated by you, your employer, or both. Items donated in the past have included [List items; e.g., gift baskets, wine, holiday décor items, food items, electronics]. I have enclosed a donation form for you to complete.

2. Please mark your calendar now and plan to attend this event on [Date]. You will receive more information in the mail. We encourage you to bring a friend and your family for a fun day at [Location].

Thank you in advance for your support of this important event, [Name]. Together we can make a difference!

Sincerely,

[Name]
Chair

From J. De Marzo, A. Gibbone, G. Letter, and C. Klein, 2012, *Healthy and sustainable fundraising activities* (Champaign, IL: Human Kinetics).

DONATION FORM

[Name of organization]

Stop, Drop, and Roll Fire Safety Event

Thank you for your contribution.
Please complete this form and fax to [Name], event chair, at [Fax number].

Donor name: _____

Organization name: _____

Mailing address: _____

_____

Phone: _____

E-mail: _____

Describe the item you are donating (please be as descriptive as possible):

_____

_____

_____

_____

_____

_____

Approximate retail value: $ _____

Thank you for your support!

From J. De Marzo, A. Gibbone, G. Letter, and C. Klein, 2012, *Healthy and sustainable fundraising activities* (Champaign, IL: Human Kinetics).

[Date]

[Name]
[Company name]
[Address]

Dear [Name],

Thank you for your generous donation of [Donated item] for the stop, drop, and roll fire safety event held on [Date] to benefit [Recipient organization].

Thanks to you and other donors like you, we doubled the number of items donated and nearly tripled the amount raised last year (from [Amount] to [Amount]). This helps in two ways:

1. [Recipient organization] will be able to [Work of recipient organization].
2. [Recipient organization] will [Another benefit to recipient organization, such as the ability to compete for a merit award].

We are planning to hold this stop, drop, and roll fire safety event again next year and again will try to increase the number of donated items and money raised for [Recipient organization]. We hope that we can count on your support for our next event.

Thank you again for your generosity, and happy holidays!

Sincerely,

[Name]
Event Chair

From J. De Marzo, A. Gibbone, G. Letter, and C. Klein, 2012, *Healthy and sustainable fundraising activities* (Champaign, IL: Human Kinetics).

THANK-YOU LETTER TO COMMUNITY ORGANIZATIONS

[Date]

[Name]
[Organization]
[Address]

Dear [Name],

Thank you for participating and supporting our stop, drop, and roll fire safety event. Thanks to your participation, we were able to raise over [Amount] for [Recipient organization].

[Recipient organization] is a not-for-profit organization that [Work of recipient organization]. The work of [Recipient organization] is supported by tax deductible contributions made by individuals, companies, and organizations.

We hope you enjoyed the stop, drop, and roll fire safety event and will plan to participate again next year. Together we can make a difference!

To your continued success,

[Name]
Event Chair

From J. De Marzo, A. Gibbone, G. Letter, and C. Klein, 2012, *Healthy and sustainable fundraising activities* (Champaign, IL: Human Kinetics).

Rubber Duck Race

Activity Description

A rubber duck race is a fun and easy family-oriented fundraiser that can be scaled to fit your group's mission or supporter base. Many charities find duck races very profitable. They add a little extra zing to the old-fashioned raffle. The event involves racing rubber ducks down a local waterway, preferably one with a good current. For a fee, supporters adopt rubber ducks for a chance at winning donated prizes. Tickets are linked to numbered ducks. All ducks are placed in the water at the starting line, and the winning duck is the one that floats to the finish line first.

Prizes can also be awarded in various categories to add to the festivities. You can even award a prize for a last place finish! Many groups organize duck races around a group outing near the waterway. In this way, a leisurely family afternoon is turned into a bigger event and fundraiser. This activity can reflect the ideals of the organization—for example, a scout group or environmental group can use a duck race to raise funds while bringing attention to environmental issues or initiatives. Groups have combined duck races with cleanup events and events in which volunteers adopt sections of the park or plant around signposts.

Additionally, you can overlap this activity with another fundraiser such as an ink cartridge drive or cell phone drive. As supporters drop off cartridges and cell phones, they can adopt a duck for the big race. Family activities can be added as well, such as an inflatable moonwalk, a face-painting booth, a temporary tattoo booth, a ball-toss game, or a dunking tank. You may choose to hold these activities on Earth Day to demonstrate to your community and participants that eco-friendly activities can be fun and strengthen communities.

Educational Objectives

Students will:

- Participate in almost every aspect of this event by using their skill sets to organize and run the race.
- Broaden their civic, health, and environmental literacy.
- Practice learning and innovation skills, media and technology skills, and many other life and career skills.

Adults will:

- Guide students through the varied roles required to navigate today's living and working environments. Specifically, they will teach them how to manage goals, work both independently and with others, and use interpersonal and problem-solving skills.

The community will:

- Benefit from increased relationships among people from various sectors of the community.
- Benefit from the modeling of prosocial behaviors such as involvement and accountability, which affect the entire community.

Targeted Dimensions of Health

Physical   **Social**   **Mental**   **Environmental**

Standards Met

National Health Education standards 1, 4, 6, and 8
National Association for Sport and Physical Education standards 1, 2, 5, and 6
21st century student outcomes:

Life and   **Learning and**   **Information, Media,**
Career Skills   **Innovation Skills**   **and Technology Skills**

21st century interdisciplinary themes: Global awareness; financial, economic, business, and entrepreneurial literacy; civic literacy; health literacy; environmental literacy

Age Level

12+

Materials

Paper for flyers
Access to computer to generate flyers and post to social networking sites
Raffle tickets
Rubber ducks
Permanent markers to number ducks
Tables for a registration area
Canoes, rowboats, or nets to collect ducks after the race

Recommended Procedures

As a stand-alone event, this activity takes just a few weeks to organize. The race itself is only a few hours long. Basically, a rubber duck race is a twist on the old-fashioned raffle. Numbered tickets that correspond to numbered ducks are sold for a small fee. The price of each duck adoption, or ticket, depends on the prizes involved, the number of supporters expected, and the amount you hope to raise. Generally, tickets range from $2 to $10. Races can be as large or small as needed. Some races have involved as few as several hundred ducks; others have involved 10,000 or more.

Adult supervisors can direct the youngest volunteers to create informational flyers either electronically or by hand, thus engaging all age groups and skill sets. Adults set up staging areas to disseminate the flyers and establish how tickets will be sold: either door to door or at a centrally located site. Young volunteers should be coached on using good communication skills when soliciting and collecting donations (e.g., proper greeting and handshaking). Here is a list of preliminary tasks:

1. Identify the location of the race.
2. Obtain permissions and permits.
3. Set the race date and possible rain date, if deemed necessary.
4. Designate a chair and possibly a co-chair, and create a procurement team and an arrangements team.
5. Identify where, when, and how tickets will be sold.
6. Determine the ticket price.
7. Create the tickets and flyers, e-mail blasts, and Facebook messages to get the word out.

Event Preparation Time Line

Three Months Prior to the Event

Begin setting up committees for your race. The following structure is recommended.

Race Chair and Co-Chair

The primary qualifications for a race chair and co-chair are a willingness to serve and an ability to lead others. The race chair is in charge of assembling the committee and leading that committee in setting ambitious and realistic goals for the race. You can have two co-chairs with equal responsibility or a chair and assistant chair, depending on what the participants want and can handle.

Because a successful rubber duck race requires a lot of work, consider dividing your event committee into two teams. A procurement team can be in charge of donated prizes, and an arrangements team can be in charge of the logistics of the race.

Procurement Team

The procurement team is in charge of soliciting race prizes. Members of this team must have the time and willingness to contact members and potential donors by phone or in person for donations. They should be friendly and persuasive. Within this team, divide members into those who solicit from members and those will solicit within the larger community.

Arrangements Team

Depending on the size of your event, you may need more than one person or a team for each of the following areas:

- Publicity. The publicity team publishes flyers, sends out e-mail blasts, posts on websites, sends out ads to local papers, makes announcements at organization functions, and sends invitations (and e-vites) to members and other community organizations.
- Setup and breakdown. This team is responsible for coordinating with the facility where the race will take place. This includes setting up tables, displaying raffle prizes or silent auction items, posting signs, attaining the rubber ducks and numbering and placing them in the water, and collecting the ducks when the race is over.

Banker or Cashier

The banker, or cashier, is responsible for collecting money from the people adopting rubber ducks. This person also determines which methods of payment will be accepted (i.e., credit cards, checks) and makes sure to have cash on hand for making change. If you decide to accept credit cards, you need to arrange a method for processing payments.

Two Months Prior to the Event

Send out a letter (via regular mail, e-mail, or both) or post a notice on your website asking for participation and contributions. Be sure to write to community businesses for donations. A well-written letter along with a donation form can help you bring in prizes for your event (see Forms and Templates). Here are a number of ways to solicit donations:

Hand out and post flyers around the community (see Forms and Templates).
Post on social networking sites.
Send e-mails to e-mail lists.
Send press releases (see Forms and Templates).
Send letters to members.
Make announcements at meetings of community organizations.
Send invitations (see Forms and Templates).

Procuring Prizes

The best ways to procure prize items is to contact members of your organization; you can also approach area businesses. The most attractive prizes are big cash prizes for first-place winners followed by smaller cash prizes for lower-level winners. It's also possible to add smaller noncash prizes, so that everyone entered has a larger chance of winning something. You can offer prize money of up to 50 percent of ticket sales and still raise a substantial sum. Half of the available prize money should be committed to the grand prize, and the balance should be used in declining amounts as you set the number of prizes (e.g., $500 for first prize, $250 for second prize, $150 for third prize, and so on).

Send out a letter (see Forms and Templates) to each of your members soliciting donations. Be sure to mention that the money raised will benefit your organization. You can suggest items to contribute as well as monetary donations to be used to purchase items such as gift baskets, sporting equipment, holiday items, stationery and gift wrap, toys, electronics, books, and autographed memorabilia. Two to four weeks after sending the letter, call members who have not responded and ask for donations.

Complete a donation form (see Forms and Templates) for each item that is donated, and give it to the setup and breakdown team. The setup team will keep track of items, establish what starting bids will be or if the item will be part of the raffle, and so on. All items should be logged; when sending out thank-you letters, you can refer to the specific item and donor. Make sure each form is filled out completely. The street address and e-mail address are important so you can send a thank-you following the event. Arrange to pick up the prizes prior to race day to be sure they make it to the event.

One Month Prior to the Event

- Determine which methods of payment you will accept. The more methods you offer, the easier it is for people to buy. Arrange to have cash on hand to make change.
- Arrange for a credit card processing machine if you will be accepting credit cards.
- Coordinate volunteers to declare the winning ducks.
- Talk it up! The more noise you make about the race, the more people you will attract.
- Send out invitations in as many forms as you can.

Selling Tickets

There are many ways to sell tickets. The simplest is having adult supervisors or responsible youngsters sell tickets as people arrive at the race. Each participant receives a numbered raffle ticket corresponding to a rubber duck.

You can also sell tickets prior to the event; you may be surprised at how many presales you will have. Groups have structured sales in blocks of 10, 20, and 100 ducks. Larger groups can easily sell several thousand tickets. You can even suggest or mandate that members of the organization or student volunteers sell a specified number of tickets prior to the event.

One or Two Weeks Before Race Day

- Make sure you have collected all the prize items.
- Confirm details with the facility where the race will take place (e.g., tables are available, waterway is accessible, volunteer lifeguards or boy scouts or girl scouts are prepared to retrieve ducks via canoes or boats, or with nets).
- Pick up any items you will need to decorate for the event.

Day of the Event

Arrive early! Set up signage, a prize table, a cashier's table, and tables for refreshments if necessary. During the race, be mindful of the time constraints; announce periodically how much time is left for ticket purchases before the start of the race. Encourage participants to donate in other ways (e.g., monetary donations). Have a participant registry to obtain e-mail and home addresses from all attendees so you can send out thank-you notes and announcements for next year's event.

Ducks can be released all at once using a fire truck cherry picker. Another option is to put them in the water as they are adopted. You can use a boom (an inflatable barrier often used to maintain oil spills) to hold the ducks back until the race begins. This may be borrowed from a local environmental department. The end of the race, or the finish line, should be clearly marked with overhead bunting if possible; if you do not have bunting, use flags. You may have an official referee stationed in a boat to identify and retrieve the winning duck(s). When the race is over, announce the winners and distribute the prizes.

After the Race

- Deposit the funds immediately.
- Send thank-you letters or e-mails to everyone who contributed a prize (see Forms and Templates).
- Send thank-you letters or e-mails to all community sponsors or organizations that assisted in the race (see Forms and Templates).
- Hold a wrap-up meeting with the race day committees to discuss what worked well and what should be changed for your next event.
- Keep a record of donors for your next event.

Postevent Processing and Evaluation

Discussion Questions for Students

Why is keeping our natural resources clean important?
Did this activity make you think differently about your environment?
How do you think this activity had an impact on the community?
What new skills did you learn from this activity?

Discussion Questions for Adults

What did you learn about mobilizing students and organizing their efforts?
What were some of the pitfalls you encountered organizing community helpers?

Was the community supportive of this event?

How could this event have been more successful?

Sustainable Extension

There are several ways to turn your duck race into an even larger moneymaker. One way is to sell food and drinks at the race. Another is to add other family-oriented fundraising activities such as inflatable bouncers, a temporary tattoo booth, a ball-toss game, or even a dunking tank.

To draw an even bigger crowd, cross-promote with other groups. Bigger events often add live auctions, silent auctions, prize raffles, sponsorships, and entertainment from a band or DJ, all of which can raise considerably more funds for your group.

Forms and Templates

Sample Flyer

Sample Press Release

Sample Newsletter Article

Sample Procurement Letter

Donation Form

Thank-You Letter to Donor

Thank-You Letter to Community Organizations

Rubber Duck Race

Please join [Name of organization] on [Date] from 9 a.m. to 12 p.m. at [Location].

All proceeds go to [Recipient organization].

Winners of the rubber duck race will receive prizes that include [List prizes; e.g., a 70-inch plasma screen TV, MP3 players, a Blu-ray disc player, dinner for two, a weekend getaway package].

Our success depends on your generosity!

From J. De Marzo, A. Gibbone, G. Letter, and C. Klein, 2012, *Healthy and sustainable fundraising activities* (Champaign, IL: Human Kinetics).

For Immediate Release

CONTACT: [Name] at [Phone number]

[Name of organization] to Hold Benefit Rubber Duck Race

[Town, State]—[Name of organization] will hold its third annual rubber duck race on [Date]. All proceeds from the event will be donated to [Recipient organization], a not-for-profit organization that [Work of the recipient organization].

The rubber duck race raised over [Amount] last year for [Recipient organization] and hopes to increase that amount this year.

The funds are used to [Describe work of recipient organization]. We are excited to be able to give back some of the programming that was cut as a result of budget constraints.

[Name of organization] is currently soliciting donations for race day prize items. If you would like to contribute or attend the rubber duck race, please contact [Name], the race day chair, at [Phone number].

From J. De Marzo, A. Gibbone, G. Letter, and C. Klein, 2012, *Healthy and sustainable fundraising activities* (Champaign, IL: Human Kinetics).

It's Rubber Duck Race Time Again!

Mark your calendar and make plans to attend [Name of organization]'s third annual rubber duck race event to be held on [Date] at [Location].

This is your chance to get outside and support [Work of recipient organization]. All proceeds from the auction will go to [Recipient organization]. Last year we raised over [Amount] for [Recipient organization] and hope to raise more this year. Plan to attend, bring a friend, and adopt a duck or two.

Also, we are still collecting prize items for the race winners. If you or your company would like to contribute to this worthwhile event, please contact [Name], the race day chair, by calling [Phone number].

From J. De Marzo, A. Gibbone, G. Letter, and C. Klein, 2012, *Healthy and sustainable fundraising activities* (Champaign, IL: Human Kinetics).

SAMPLE PROCUREMENT LETTER

[Date]

[Name and title]
[Company name]
[Address]

Dear [Name],

I would like to invite you to participate in a very special event. For the third year in a row, [Name of organization] will be holding a rubber duck race at [Location] on [Date] to benefit [Recipient organization], and we need your help to make it a success.

All proceeds will be donated to [Recipient organization], a not-for-profit organization that [Work of the recipient organization].

The work of [Recipient organization] is supported by tax deductible contributions made by individuals, companies, and organizations.

Here's how you can help:

1. Please consider contributing a prize item to the rubber duck race. The item can be donated by you, your employer, or both. In the past, donors have donated [List items; e.g., gift baskets, wine, holiday décor items, food items, electronics]. I have enclosed a donation form for you to complete.

2. Please mark your calendar now and plan to attend the rubber duck race on [Date]. You will receive more information in the mail. We encourage you to bring a friend and your family for a fun day at [Location].

Thank you in advance for your support of this important event, [Name]. Together we can make a difference!

Sincerely,

[Name]
Race Chair

From J. De Marzo, A. Gibbone, G. Letter, and C. Klein, 2012, *Healthy and sustainable fundraising activities* (Champaign, IL: Human Kinetics).

[Name of organization]

Rubber Duck Race

Thank you for making a contribution to our rubber duck race. Please complete this form and fax to [Name], race chair, at [Fax number].

Donor name: _____

Organization name: _____

Mailing address: _____

_____

Phone: _____

E-mail: _____

Describe the item you are donating (please be as descriptive as possible):

_____

_____

_____

_____

_____

_____

Approximate retail value: $ _____

Thank you for your support!

[Date]

[Name]
[Company]
[Address]

Dear [Name],

Thank you for your generous donation of [Donated item] for the rubber duck race held on [Date] to benefit [Recipient organization].

Thanks to you and other donors like you, we doubled the number of items donated and nearly tripled the amount we raised last year (from [Amount] to [Amount]). This helps in two ways:

1. [Recipient organization] will be able to continue to support [Work of recipient organization].

2. [Recipient organization] will also [Add another benefit, such as the ability to compete for a merit award].

We are planning to hold this rubber duck race again next year and again will try to increase the number of donated items and money raised for [Recipient organization]. We hope that we can count on your support for our next event.

Thank you again for your generosity, and happy holidays!

Sincerely,

[Name]
Rubber Duck Race Chair

From J. De Marzo, A. Gibbone, G. Letter, and C. Klein, 2012, *Healthy and sustainable fundraising activities* (Champaign, IL: Human Kinetics).

[Date]

[Name]
[Title]
[Address]

Dear [Name],

Thank you for attending our [Month] meeting and participating and supporting our rubber duck race. Thanks to your participation, we were able to raise over [Amount] for [Recipient organization].

[Recipient organization], a not-for-profit organization, [Describe the work of recipient organization].

The work of [Recipient organization] is supported by tax deductible contributions made by individuals, companies, and organizations.

We hope you enjoyed the rubber duck race and will plan to participate again next year. Together we can make a difference!

To your continued success,

[Name]
[Year] Race Chair

From J. De Marzo, A. Gibbone, G. Letter, and C. Klein, 2012, *Healthy and sustainable fundraising activities* (Champaign, IL: Human Kinetics).

Silent Auction

Activity Description

A silent auction can be very lucrative when conducted properly; in this case, size and organization matter. This event takes more planning and organized efforts than the previous activities; however, young volunteers organized into teams can be of tremendous help. The more help you can get with this activity, the bigger your profits will be.

This activity can reflect your organization's mission; for example, you may choose to auction off only services and material items that are green, or earth friendly, such as one month of eco-friendly lawn care, $100 worth of eco-responsible dry cleaning services, or one total home cleaning service with eco-friendly cleaning supplies. In this way, you can teach youngsters that they do not have to compromise their beliefs or ideals to make a profit. This activity is loaded with opportunities to learn and practice 21st century skills.

Educational Objectives

Students will:

- Increase their global awareness and financial, economic, and entrepreneurial literacy.
- Increase their health and environmental literacy.
- Broaden their learning and increase their innovation skills by focusing on creativity, communication, and collaboration.
- Get firsthand exposure to the complexities of a work environment and learn the value of problem-solving skills and clear communication.

Adults will:

- Recreate today's life and work environment to help young people develop necessary skills such as flexibility, self-direction, team building, productivity, accountability, and leadership.

The community will:

- Benefit from young people being taught the skills necessary to be productive citizens in today's challenging world.
- Benefit from citizens modeling prosocial and socially responsible civic behavior to young people.

Targeted Dimensions of Health

Social   **Mental**   **Emotional**   **Environmental**

Standards Met

National Health Education standards 3, 4, 5, 6, 7, and 8
National Association for Sport and Physical Education standard 5

21st century student outcomes:

**Life and
Career Skills**

**Learning and
Innovation Skills**

**Information, Media,
and Technology Skills**

21st century interdisciplinary themes: Global awareness; financial, economic, business, and entrepreneurial literacy; civic literacy; health literacy; environmental literacy

Age Level

12+

Materials

Paper for flyers and posters
Access to the Internet for e-mail blasts and social networking posts
Access to local and community newspapers
Tables
Signage for identifying auction items

Recommended Procedures

Silent auctions are a popular way to raise funds; most people are familiar with how they work and tend to be less intimidated by them than they are by live auctions. In a silent auction, items are placed on display and bidders can sign a sheet with their name or bidder number and a bidding amount. The winner of the auctioned item is the person with the highest bid at the end of the auction.

An auction provides a way for people to support your organization (a good cause) and get something valuable in return. Silent auctions are scalable: you can have as few as a dozen good items and see a profit. A small auction can be planned and executed by just two or three people. Lastly, silent auctions can easily be incorporated into larger events. Most events that are held indoors can include a silent auction.

Event Preparation Time Line

Three Months Prior to the Event

Setting a Date

Holding your auction on the same day as another event can be very lucrative. Groups have doubled their fundraising profits by holding a silent auction on Back to School Night or during PTA elections, a holiday gift boutique, and even a 3v3 basketball tournament. Determine a date that works well for your organization and its members and that will result in the greatest participation.

Organizing the Auction Committee

Your first task is to designate a person to chair the auction committee. The primary qualifications of the auction chair are a willingness to serve and an ability to lead others. This person assembles the committee and leads that committee in setting ambitious and realistic goals for the auction. For larger auctions, you may want to divide your committee into two teams. A procurement team can focus on procuring auction items, and an arrangements team can focus on the logistics of the auction.

Procurement Team

The procurement team solicits contributions to the auction. These people must have the time and willingness to contact members and potential donors by phone or in person for donations. They should be friendly and persuasive. Divide this team into those who solicit from member and those who solicit within the larger community.

Arrangements Team

Depending on the size of your event, you may need more than one person or a team for each of the following areas:

- Publicity. The publicity team publishes flyers, sends out e-mail blasts, posts on websites, sends out ads to local papers, makes announcements at organization functions, and sends invitations (and e-vites) to members.
- Setup. This group is responsible for coordinating with the facility where the auction will take place, including setting up tables, displaying auction items, posting signs, and placing bid sheets with each item.

Banker or Cashier

The banker, or cashier, is responsible for totaling up each purchaser's bill and collecting money. This person also determines which methods of payment will be accepted (i.e., credit cards, checks) and makes sure to have cash on hand for making change. If you decide to accept credit cards, you will need to arrange a method for processing payments.

Two Months Prior to the Event

Send out a letter (via regular mail, e-mail, or both) or post a notice on your website asking for participation and contributions. Be sure to write to community businesses for donations. A well-written letter along with a donation form can help you bring in items for your auction (see Forms and Templates). Here are a number of ways to solicit donations:

Hand out and post flyers around the community (see Forms and Templates).
Post on social networking sites.
Send e-mails to e-mail lists.
Send press releases (see Forms and Templates).
Send letters to members.
Make announcements at meetings.
Send invitations (see Forms and Templates).

Procuring Auction Items

The best ways to procure items is to contact members of your organization; you can also approach area businesses.

- Send out a letter (see Forms and Templates) to each of your members soliciting donations. Be sure to mention that the money raised will benefit your organization. You can suggest items that they can contribute and suggest that monetary donations will be used to purchase auction items such as gift baskets, sporting equipment, holiday items, stationery and gift wrap, toys, electronics, books, and autographed memorabilia.

- Two to four weeks after sending the letter, phone members who have not responded and ask for donations.
- Complete a donation form (see Forms and Templates) for each item and give it to the setup team. The setup team will keep track of items, establish what starting bids will be or if the item will be part of the raffle, and so on. All items should be logged; when sending out thank-you letters, you can refer to the specific item and donor. Make sure the form is filled out completely. Street and e-mail addresses are important so you can send a thank-you letter following the auction. The value of donated items is helpful for establishing the bid amounts.

Arrange to pick up the items prior to the auction to minimize the possibility of their not making it to the event.

One Month Prior to the Event

Talk it up! The more noise you make concerning your event, the more people you will attract. Send out invitations to the auction in as many forms as you can.

One or Two Weeks Before the Event

- Make sure you have collected all donated items.
- Determine which methods of payment you will accept. The more methods you offer, the easier it is for people to buy. Arrange to have cash on hand to make change.
- Arrange for a credit card processing machine if you will be accepting credit cards.
- Coordinate volunteers to tally winning bids.
- Confirm details with the facility where the auction will be held (e.g., tables are available, floor plan is appropriate).
- Create bid forms (see Forms and Templates).
- Pick up any items you will need to decorate for the event.

Setting Bid Prices

The general rule of thumb for setting bid prices is to start the bidding at 50 percent of the value of the item. The bidding increases from there in increments of 10 percent of the value (for convenience, you can round). For example, for an item valued at $50, the bidding starts at $25 and increases in increments of $5.

Day of the Event

Arrive early! Set up tables, including the cashier's table. Pay attention to how you arrange items on the tables. Make them as attractive as possible and think about placing similar items together or separate, depending on the items. Set bid sheets out with the items, and make sure you have a pen at each bid sheet. During the auction, be mindful of the time constraints; announce periodically how much time is left for bidding. Encourage participants to donate in other ways (e.g., monetary donations). Have a participant registry to obtain e-mail and home addresses from all attendees so you can send out thank-you notes and announcements of next year's event.

After the auction tables close, gather up all bid sheets and tally the results. While this is happening, you can hold a raffle for another item or have people from your organization speak or entertain the participants. Establish a method for tallying bids before the event with your banking team. When the results have been tallied, announce the winners, collect payments, and distribute the items.

After the Auction

- Deposit the funds immediately.
- Send thank-you letters to everyone who contributed an item to the auction (see Forms and Templates).
- Send thank-you letters to everyone who purchased something at the auction.
- Hold a wrap-up meeting with the auction committee to discuss what worked well and what should be changed for your next auction.
- Keep a record of donors for your next event.

Postevent Processing and Evaluation

Discussion Questions for Students

How has your involvement in the silent auction improved your innovation skills? What types of information, media, and technology skills did you use to organize this event? What other 21st century skills did you practice while taking part in this activity?

Discussion Questions for Adults

Has this activity increased students' financial, economic, and entrepreneurial literacy? Could this activity be used to expand student or community global awareness in any way?

Sustainable Extension

You might want to hold this event on its own or in conjunction with another event, or at any gathering at which patrons will be waiting or have down time to shop. If you have many items, you can host the auction on its own and have members of your organization present the mission or work on recruitment of potential new volunteers or participants.

Forms and Templates

Sample Flyer
Sample Press Release
Sample Newsletter Article
Sample Procurement Letter
Sample Donation Form
Sample Bid Sheet
Thank-You Letter to Donor
Thank-You Letter to Bidders

Silent Auction

Please Join [Name of organization] on [Date] from
7 to 9 p.m. [Location].

All proceeds go to [Recipient organization].

Auction items include [List items; e.g., holiday decorations, gift items, electronics, gift certificates for community services, dinner for two, a weekend getaway package].

Please contact [Name] at [Phone number] to donate auction items for this event. Our success depends on your generosity!

From J. De Marzo, A. Gibbone, G. Letter, and C. Klein, 2012, *Healthy and sustainable fundraising activities* (Champaign, IL: Human Kinetics).

For Immediate Release

CONTACT [Name] at [Phone number]

[Name of organization] to Hold Benefit Auction

[Town, State]—[Name of organization] will hold an annual silent auction on [Date]. All proceeds from the auction will be donated to [Recipient organization], a not-for-profit organization that [Work of recipient organization].

The silent auction raised over [Amount] last year for [Recipient organization] and hopes to increase that amount this year.

The funds are used to [Work of recipient organization]. We are excited to be able to give back some of the programming that was cut as a result of budget constraints.

[Name of organization] is currently soliciting donations for auction items. If you would like to contribute or attend the auction, please contact [Name], auction chair, at [Phone number].

From J. De Marzo, A. Gibbone, G. Letter, and C. Klein, 2012, *Healthy and sustainable fundraising activities* (Champaign, IL: Human Kinetics).

It's Silent Auction Time Again!

Mark your calendar and make plans to attend [Name of organization]'s annual silent auction to be held on [Date] during [Name of other event; e.g., PTA elections].

This is your chance to get a jump on holiday shopping and support [Work of recipient organization]. All proceeds from the auction will go to [Recipient organization]. Last year we raised over [Amount] for [Recipient organization] and hope to raise more this year. Plan to attend the auction, bring a friend, and bring your checkbook!

Also, we are still collecting items for the auction. If you or your company would like to contribute to this worthwhile event, please contact [Name], auction chair, by calling [Phone number].

From J. De Marzo, A. Gibbone, G. Letter, and C. Klein, 2012, *Healthy and sustainable fundraising activities* (Champaign, IL: Human Kinetics).

[Date]

[Name and title]
[Company name]
[Address]

Dear [Name],

I would like to invite you to participate in a very special event. For the [Number] year in a row, [Name of organization] will be holding a silent auction at [Location or name of other event] to benefit [Recipient organization], and we need your help to make it a success.

All proceeds from the auction will be donated to [Recipient organization], a not-for-profit organization that [Work of recipient organization].

The work of [Recipient organization] is supported by tax deductible contributions made by individuals, companies, and organizations.

Here's how you can help:

1. Please consider contributing an item to the silent auction. The item can be donated by you, your employer, or both. Items that have sold well at past auctions include [List items; e.g., gift baskets, wine, holiday décor items, any food items, books]. I have enclosed a donation form for you to complete.

2. Please mark your calendar now and plan to attend the auction on [Date]. The auction will be held in conjunction with [Other event; e.g. PTA meeting] at [Location]. You will receive more information in the mail. We encourage you to bring a friend or colleague and your checkbook.

Thank you in advance for your support of this important event, [Name]. Together we can make a difference!

Sincerely,

[Name]
Auction Chair

From J. De Marzo, A. Gibbone, G. Letter, and C. Klein, 2012, *Healthy and sustainable fundraising activities* (Champaign, IL: Human Kinetics).

[Name of organization],

Silent Auction to Benefit [Recipient organization]

Thank you for making a contribution to our silent auction. Please complete this form and fax to [Name], auction chair, at [Fax number].

Donor name: _____

Organization name: _____

Mailing address: _____

_____

Phone: _____

E-mail: _____

Describe the item you are donating (please be as descriptive as possible):

_____

_____

_____

_____

_____

_____

Approximate retail value: $ _____

Thank you for your support!

SAMPLE BID SHEET

[Name of organization]

Silent Auction: [Date]

To benefit [Recipient organization]

Item: _____

_____

Donor: _____

Retail value: $_____

Minimum bid: $_____

Bid increments: Minimum increase of $_____

Guaranteed bid price: $_____

Name	Bid

From J. De Marzo, A. Gibbone, G. Letter, and C. Klein, 2012, *Healthy and sustainable fundraising activities* (Champaign, IL: Human Kinetics).

THANK-YOU LETTER TO DONOR

[Date]

[Name]
[Company]
[Address]

Dear [Name],

Thank you for your generous donation of the [Donated item] for the silent auction held at [Event or location] to benefit [Recipient organization].

Thanks to you and other donors like you, we doubled the number of items donated and nearly tripled the amount raised last year (from [Amount] to [Amount]). This helps in two ways:

1. [Recipient organization] will be able to continue to [Work of recipient organization].

2. [Recipient organization] will also [List another benefit; e.g., the ability to compete for a merit award].

We are planning to hold this silent auction again next year and again will try to increase the number of donated items and money raised for [Recipient organization]. We hope that we can count on your support for our next event.

Thank you again for your generosity, and happy holidays!

Sincerely,

[Name]
[Year] Auction Chair

From J. De Marzo, A. Gibbone, G. Letter, and C. Klein, 2012, *Healthy and sustainable fundraising activities* (Champaign, IL: Human Kinetics).

THANK-YOU LETTER TO BIDDERS

[Date]

[Name]
[Company or affiliation]
[Address]

Dear [Name],

Thank you for attending [Event] and participating in our silent auction. Thanks to your participation, we were able to raise over [Amount] for [Recipient organization].

[Recipient organization] is a not-for-profit organization that [Work of recipient organization].

The work of [Recipient organization] is supported by tax deductible contributions made by individuals, companies, and organizations.

We hope you enjoyed the auction and will plan to participate again next year. Together we can make a difference!

To your continued success,

[Name]
[Year] Auction Chair

From J. De Marzo, A. Gibbone, G. Letter, and C. Klein, 2012, *Healthy and sustainable fundraising activities* (Champaign, IL: Human Kinetics).

MIDLEVEL FUNDRAISERS

Require increased level of technological know-how and increased youth supervision

The activities in this chapter are a step above those in chapter 3. They require a higher level of knowledge, skills, and abilities from your members, and some require an increased level of technological know-how. Young volunteers require more supervision in some of these activities, and adult volunteers may have to seek assistance outside of their immediate groups to create a successful fundraiser.

Bowling for Bucks

Activity Description

Bowling for bucks raises low to moderate funds while promoting community wellness. Using the Nintendo Wii gaming system and the AMF Bowling Pinbusters game (or other compatible gaming system and game), you can hold a bowling tournament. The tournament can be open to all students or members of your organization and their families. In the process, young people learn life skills by working with community members and helping with event planning, design, and management. Traditional bowling establishments may be substituted for the video game if preferred. Bowling for bucks is set up as a tournament where participants compete for prizes. Entry fees or sponsorship donations are the funding sources.

Educational Objectives

Students will:

- Create advertisements on the computer (increasing their technological literacy) or by hand and disseminate information about the event. They will increase their involvement in the school or organization and in the larger community through their participation.
- Create participation stickers and labels.
- Create and manage tournament details.
- Assist participants with the video gaming equipment.

Adults will:

- Model socially responsible behavior as well as care and concern for community neighbors.

The community will:

- Benefit from your organization's interest in promoting socially responsible behavior and community engagement.
- Experience increased cohesiveness from citizens working together.

Targeted Dimensions of Health

Social

Mental

Emotional

Spiritual

Standards Met

National Health Education standards 1, 2, 4, 6, and 7
National Association for Sport and Physical Education standards 1, 2, and 5
21st century student outcomes:

Life and Career Skills

Learning and Innovation Skills

Information, Media, and Technology Skills

21st century interdisciplinary themes: Financial, economic, business, and entrepreneurial literacy; civic literacy; health literacy; environmental literacy

Age Level

10+

Materials

Paper for flyers and posters
Access to the Internet
Access to local and community newspapers
Premade stickers, permission passes, or pins
Video gaming system and video game

Recommended Procedures

1. Choose the date of the event.
2. Identify the recipient organization if you are sharing the donations.
3. Identify donation site(s) for prizes or sponsorships (e.g., local library, grocery store, strip mall).
4. Create flyers either electronically or by hand. Develop an automated message for a phone blast.
5. Distribute flyers within the organization or send e-mails or an automatic phone message. Canvas the community to distribute flyers or post announcements around the community.
6. Identify an entry fee collection procedure if the tournament is taking place in a school setting. This can be done very simply by having adult supervisors or responsible students collect donations as students enter the school building on the designated day.
7. Sponsorship donations can also be collected prior to the event. A few days before the event, volunteers can collect donations as well as a week prior to the event at centrally located community sites, schools, or during organization meetings or events.

Young volunteers should be coached on using good communication skills when soliciting and collecting sponsorship donations.

Event Preparation Time Line

This event can be conducted in as little as a month. The initial brainstorming committee meeting can commence earlier if desired.

Four Weeks Prior to the Event

Meet with your committee to brainstorm ideas about the tournament, assign jobs (e.g., DJ, volunteers, prize solicitors) and make a time line. Determine the entry fee (e.g., $10, which includes two practice games and a single-elimination tournament). You may decide to provide refreshments for an additional cost. Determine the tournament style and scoring system. You can use websites to help you such as www.printyourbrackets.com/bowlingbrackets.html, which creates tournament brackets based on the type of game and tournament style you select.

Create an e-mail message or flyer that briefly explains who (your organization) is doing what (holding a bowling for bucks tournament), and why (e.g., to raise funds for a class trip or local organization) and when (include the date, time, and location of the event and where contributions are being collected). Young volunteers can create the flyer or e-mail message with appropriate word processing software. If you are collecting donations within the community, check to see whether permission is required. Always provide an alternate means of contribution (e.g., monetary donations or donations of needed supplies). The flyer should also include the entry fee of the event. As always, children should be escorted or chaperoned through neighborhoods when posting flyers for the event.

Determine volunteers to solicit prizes and brainstorm potential funding sources (e.g., local businesses, organizations).

Three Weeks Prior to the Event

Flyers, e-mail blasts, and phone calls via automated service should be distributed at this time. If your event will include the whole community, you can alert the public through advertisements in local papers and via signage at local commercial sites. Community events may require broader advertising and varied donation sites to be successful. Flyers can be posted on the school district or organization website and social networking sites. Local businesses can be asked to participate by providing a donation for a raffle to be held during the tournament.

Two Weeks Prior to the Event

If your tournament is taking place in a school or work environment, have participants purchase a button or lanyard with a tag that says: *I contributed to Bowling for Bucks for [Recipient organization]—You In?* Some people will donate more than the suggested amount, and it gives those that do not want to be participants an opportunity to contribute to the cause.

Create tournament style and scoring systems and review jobs, which include helping out with registration, setting up Wii consoles, facilitating the game, serving refreshments, updating brackets, deejaying, and providing supervision or security. Young volunteers can be responsible for creating brackets for the event.

One Week Prior to the Event

Meet with the crew to confirm event day procedures.

Day of the Event

On the day of the event, all volunteers should report early to set up. The video game systems will need to be set up and tested. Brackets will need to be posted for displaying scores and reporting winners. Refreshments tables and DJ equipment need to be set up as well, if applicable. At the conclusion of the event, the cleanup team is responsible for cleaning up.

After the Event

Thank-you letters should be sent out promptly following the event to all contributors.

Postevent Processing and Evaluation

A point system can be incorporated as an evaluation for those involved in the management and orchestration of the event. A sample rubric is a simple way to provide a description of behaviors that can be assessed for an individual (table 4.1). For example, students can earn points toward a grade or toward a goal as instructed by their teacher, coach, or club supervisor.

Discussion Questions for Students

How did your participation affect the success of the event?

Did you model socially responsible behavior?

What aspects of the event can be improved for a similar event in the future?

Discussion Questions for Adults

What did you learn about mobilizing students, organizations, and communities?
Was the community, school, or workplace supportive of this event?
How might this event have been more successful?

Sustainable Extension

Bowling is a lifetime activity that can be enjoyed by a variety of age levels and abilities. Participation in this activity can continue throughout the year and the event can be offered on multiple occasions.

Table 4.1   Point-Earning Rubric

Assessment areas	Three points	Two points	One point
Involvement	• Participates in all activities. • Contributes to each step of the process: brainstorming, organizing, implementing. • Shares and produces all required items individually and as a group member. • Assesses personal gains from participation and connects gains to the service experience.	• Participates in most activities. • Contributes to two steps of the process: brainstorming, organizing, implementing. • Shares and produces some required items individually and as a group member. • Assesses personal gains from participation or reflects on the service experience.	• Participates in some activities. • Contributes to one step of the process: brainstorming, organizing, implementing. • Shares and produces required items individually or as a group member. • Does not report personal gains or a connection to the service experience.
Community connections	• Personal contribution applies directly to community service. • Uses organizational, leadership, and interpersonal skills within the community project. • Provides evidence of how the work advanced the goals of the project.	• Personal contribution applies to community service. • Uses organizational, leadership, and interpersonal skills occasionally within the community project. • Provides evidence of work that does not connect to advancing the goals of the project.	• Personal contribution does not apply directly to community service. • Does not use organizational, leadership, and interpersonal skills within the community project. • Does not provide evidence of how the work advanced the goals of the project.
Civic responsibility	• Demonstrates responsible behavior and a concern for others at all times; acts as a model citizen. • Works well with others.	• Considers the well-being of others and the group; is sensitive and responsive. • Works with others.	• Demonstrates self-direction and independence. • Does not work well with others.
Professionalism	• Arrives on time at all meetings. • Completes all requirements in a timely manner.	• Arrives late to one meeting or event. • Completes most requirements in a timely manner.	• Arrives late to two or more meetings or events. • Does not complete most requirements in a timely manner.

Video Game Sport Competition

Activity Description

You can bring video game sport competition to a new level by holding a competition in a social environment. Bringing students and their family members and friends together to participate in a fundraiser that includes popular video games provides a recreational sporting activity that can be enjoyed by all. This event can generate low to moderate funds and can take place on a single day or over multiple days. The intention is to draw those that enjoy video gaming, supervisory adults, and community patrons together in an activity that promotes physical activity and social recreation.

Educational Objectives

Students will:

- Create advertisements on the computer (increasing their technological literacy) or by hand and disseminate information for the event, which will increase their involvement in the school or organization and in the larger community.
- Create and manage tournament details.
- Assist participants with video gaming equipment.
- Compile music for the event.

Adults will:

- Model socially responsible behavior as well as care and concern for neighbors.

The community will:

- Benefit from your organization's encouragement of socially responsible behavior and community engagement.
- Experience increased cohesiveness from citizens working together.

Targeted Dimensions of Health

Social   **Mental**   **Emotional**   **Spiritual**

Standards Met

National Health Education standards 1, 2, 4, 7, and 8
National Association for Sport and Physical Education standards 1, 2, 5, and 6
21st century student outcomes:

**Life and
Career Skills**   **Learning and
Innovation Skills**   **Information, Media,
and Technology Skills**

21st century interdisciplinary themes: Financial, economic, business, and entrepreneurial literacy; civic literacy; health literacy; environmental literacy

Age Level

10+

Materials

Paper for flyers and posters
Access to the Internet
Access to local and community newspapers
Music or a DJ
Gaming systems and games
Refreshments
Raffle tickets

Recommended Procedures

1. Hold an event committee meeting.
2. Meet with people from other departments or organizations for help with technology and facility setup.
3. Create an event flyer and sign-up sheets.
4. Secure donations.
5. Recruit volunteers.
6. Review the physical setup and discuss the type of brackets (e.g., single versus double elimination, blind draw versus seeded; refer to www.printyourbrackets.com/10teamdoubleelimination.html).
7. Arrange for event setup and cleanup.

Event Preparation Time Line

Six Weeks Prior to the Event

Meet with the event committee to decide who is working on the jobs and to establish deadlines. A school technology staff member should be invited to attend because this event will require the use of electronic equipment. Jobs include setting up and cleaning up, arranging music, supervising stations, keeping records, selling refreshments, preparing lists of registered names for each sport, and collecting raffle tickets.

At this point you also want to map out the night and create brackets. Students and teachers create the brackets once all of the students have signed up; they use the brackets at www.printyourbrackets.com. Students advance if they have the higher score in their bracket. Remember, the purpose of the event is for everyone to have fun and get some fitness in; if you had fun, you won!

Five Weeks Prior to the Event

This is the time to create flyers and sign-up sheets to post and e-mail. Participants will need to identify the activity they wish to participate in (e.g., boxing, soccer, beach volleyball, table tennis). The flyer should include the following:

- An announcement of the event and the recipient of the funds raised (e.g., physical education department).

- A list of video gaming system sports to choose from (e.g. boxing, soccer, beach volleyball, table tennis).
- The date of the event.
- The deadline for signing up and where to sign up. The deadline should be two weeks prior to the event.
- The tournament cost (e.g., $10 to enter and play, which includes a ticket for one free slice of pizza and one free drink; $5 for those attending only to watch).
- Participants can also pay per sport (e.g., $4 per sport $\times$ 5 sports = $20 for full entry).

Four Weeks Prior to the Event

Students canvas the community (e.g., stores, restaurants) asking for donations of either refreshments or gift cards or prizes that can be raffled off.

Students should be responsible for finding other students who play in a band or who can deejay. The band performs only for the first portion of the event before the gaming begins and during intermissions. The school can use funds to purchase or rent game systems to be used for this and other events or during the school day. Also, participants can be invited to bring their own system and receive a discount for doing so. You will need to know who is bringing systems beforehand to make sure you have enough game stations. Students must also find volunteers to help out with the event.

Three Weeks Prior to the Event

Set up a meeting to get a report on donations, volunteers, equipment, and the DJ.

Two Weeks Prior to the Event

Set up a meeting to get a report on donations and volunteers and to confirm the availability of the equipment and DJ.

One Week Prior to the Event

A week before the event, you should hold a final organizational meeting to be sure everything is taken care of. Any last-minute changes or additions should be discussed at this meeting.

Day of the Event

The day of the event, students should arrive early to set up the available equipment. Any equipment participants may be bringing will need to be set up once they arrive, which should not take much time. Stations for specific sports should be set up and labeled accordingly (e.g., five stations each for boxing, beach volleyball, soccer, and table tennis). Participants should be allowed to play only the sport(s) they registered and paid for. Volunteers in charge of refreshments and music should set up their areas. Once the night has ended, the cleanup crew is responsible for staying and cleaning up.

Postevent Processing and Evaluation

Discussion Questions for Students

Were there any equipment issues and how can they be addressed?
How can attendance be increased for a future event?
Were there any complaints and how were they addressed?

Discussion Questions for Adults

How was the event effective and efficient?
Were refreshments and other items well received?
Were raffle prizes well received?

Sustainable Extension

In order to encourage daily physical activity, active video games can be used for recreation and enjoyment. Typical sports tournaments may exclude those that are not skilled enough to compete or who have inhibitions. Active video gaming can accommodate a more inclusive population of participants and provide an alternative or addition to a traditional competitive sporting event.

Forms and Templates

Video Game Tournament Registration Form

VIDEO GAME TOURNAMENT REGISTRATION FORM

Registration deadline:_____

Team name (if applicable): _____

Player 1 full name:_____
Address: _____
City, state, zip: _____
Phone number:_____
E-mail address: _____

Player 2 full name:_____
Address: _____
City, state, zip: _____
Phone number:_____
E-mail address: _____

Player 3 full name:_____
Address: _____
City, state, zip: _____
Phone number:_____
E-mail address: _____

Player 4 full name:_____
Address: _____
City, state, zip: _____
Phone number:_____
E-mail address: _____

Other players (if applicable): _____
_____
_____

Entry fee:_____

Registration is on a first come, first served basis. Both the registration form and the entry fee must be submitted in order to reserve a spot in the tournament. Once the tournament brackets are full, tournament entries will no longer be accepted.

From J. De Marzo, A. Gibbone, G. Letter, and C. Klein, 2012, *Healthy and sustainable fundraising activities* (Champaign, IL: Human Kinetics).

Goalball: Fun for All

Activity Description

Goalball fundraisers are generally organized to raise money for the United States Association for Blind Athletes. In the process, volunteers learn life skills by working with community members and planning, designing, and managing the tournament.

Goalball was invented in 1946 by an Austrian, Hanz Lorenzen, and a German, Sepp Reindl. It was used for sport and rehabilitation post–World War II, specifically for blind veterans. It became an official Paralympic sport at the Arnhem 1980 Paralympics Games. Goalball is now a game predominantly played by those with visual impairments. All participants are required to wear blindfolds, even if they are completely blind, to ensure an even playing field. Monies are raised through team registration and event purchases.

Goalball is played by two teams of three players with a maximum of three substitutes for each team. The game is played in a gymnasium on a court 18 by 9 meters, which is divided into two halves by a center line (see figure 4.1). The goals extend across the length of the 9-meter ends of the court. The strategies include throwing, blocking, and anticipation. The rules and setup are simple, and the game can be played by all types of people. Any time the ball is in play and completely crosses a goal line, a goal is scored. The team with the most goals at the end of the playing time is the winner. The playing time is 14 minutes total (two 7-minute halves) with a 3-minute break to change ends during the half.

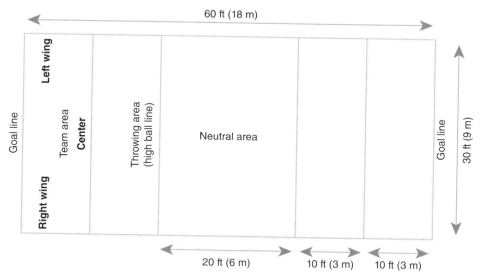

Figure 4.1   Setup for the game of goalball.

Objective of the Game

Roll the ball in a bowling motion so that it completely crosses over the opposing team's goal line, scoring a point.

Rules

- Blindfolds: All team members must wear blindfolds at all times during the game.
- Time limits: Upon receiving control of the ball, the team has only eight seconds to roll the ball back toward the opposing team in an attempt to score.
- Rolling: The ball must be rolled, or bowled, on the floor rather than thrown.
- Dead ball: When the ball has stopped moving and the players are unaware of its location, it is returned to the closest player, usually the winger.
- Out: When the ball rolls over the outside lines, it is turned over to the other team.

Official goalball rules from the International Blind Sports Federation: www.ibsa.es/eng/deportes/goalball/IBSA-Goalball-Rules-2010-2013.pdf

Educational Objectives

Students will:

- Create advertisements on the computer (increasing their technological literacy) or by hand and disseminate information for the event, which will increase their involvement in the school or organization and in the larger community.
- Create and manage tournament details.
- Design event T-shirts.
- Learn the rules and regulations of goalball.

Adults will:

- Model socially responsible behavior as well as care and concern for neighbors.

The community will:

- Benefit from your organization's interest in promoting socially responsible behavior and community engagement.
- Experience increased cohesiveness from citizens working together.

Targeted Dimensions of Health

| Social | Mental | Emotional | Spiritual |

Standards Met

National Health Education standards 1, 2, 4, 6, and 7
National Association for Sport and Physical Education standards 1, 2, and 5
21st century student outcomes:

| Life and Career Skills | Learning and Innovation Skills | Information, Media, and Technology Skills |

21st century interdisciplinary themes: Financial, economic, business, and entrepreneurial literacy; civic literacy; health literacy; environmental literacy

Age Level

10+

Materials

Paper for flyers and posters
Access to the Internet
Access to local and community newspapers
Equipment needed to play: goalballs, knee and elbow pads, blindfolds

Recommended Procedures

1. Hold a tournament committee meeting.
2. Choose a date.
3. Create flyers.
4. Create brackets for the tournament.
5. Create a design for the T-shirts to award to the championship team.
6. Brainstorm about how to buy discounted T-shirts or have them donated.
7. Establish jobs for committee members or teams.

Event Preparation Time Line

Three Months Prior to the Event

Hold your first tournament committee meeting, choose an event manager (or managers), and decide how many teams will be allowed to enter. You must also decide how much to charge each team to compete as well as your target population. After deciding how many teams you are allowing to compete (e.g., seven; first come, first served), create your tournament brackets. For help creating brackets, go to www.printyourbrackets.com.

The next task is to determine how you will inform your target population about the tournament (e.g., flyers, e-mail). Flyers should be eye catching (colorful and creative) and include the name of your tournament and the date, time, and place. Also include the cost per team to compete and the number of players allowed on a team. Finally, be sure to provide the name, e-mail address, and phone number of the event manager. Young volunteers can create the flyers using their favorite computer program.

Assign people to the various tasks such as registration, handling money, and being the primary contact. In the Forms and Templates section, you will find a time sheet with a list of jobs that need to be done. Volunteers write their names under the jobs they have committed to and the time slots they have chosen. Shifts are one hour long, and volunteers should sign up for two of them, either back to back or with a break between them. Also, goalball tournaments often provide T-shirts to the winning team. Consider having young volunteers design the shirts.

Two Months Prior to the Event

Making arrangements for the tournament involves finding out when your venue (e.g., gym) is available (days and times). Contact the person in charge of the venue (e.g., school athletic director). Explain exactly when and for how long you will need the space (e.g., for at least five hours on either a Saturday or Sunday). You also need to obtain equipment and setup materials. If you decide to provide refreshments, decide what you will include and a refreshment-selling team will need to be established.

Volunteers will need to learn all aspects of the game and how to run the tournament. All those involved can practice the game and review all the components during practice sessions. Youtube videos can be used as visual demonstrations of the game.

Three Weeks Prior to the Event

Flyers, e-mail blasts, and phone calls via automated service should be distributed at this time. If your event will include the whole community, you can alert the public through advertisements in local papers and via signage at local commercial sites. Community events may require broader advertising and varied donation sites to be successful. Flyers can be posted on the school district or organization website and social networking sites. Local businesses can be asked to participate by providing a donation for a raffle to be held during the tournament.

Two Weeks Prior to the Event

Create tournament style and scoring systems and review jobs, which include helping out with registration, setting up, facilitating the game, serving refreshments, updating brackets, deejaying, and providing supervision or security. Young volunteers can be responsible for creating brackets for the event.

One Week Prior to the Event

Meet with the crew to confirm event day procedures.

Day of the Event

On the day of the event, all volunteers should report early to set up. Brackets will need to be posted for displaying scores and reporting winners. Refreshments tables and equipment need to be set up as well, if applicable. At the conclusion of the event, the cleanup team is responsible for cleaning up.

After the Event

Thank-you letters should be sent out promptly following the event to all contributors.

Postevent Processing and Evaluation

Provide those involved with an anonymous feedback form to complete and return. Suggested questions include:

- What aspects of the event made it a success?
- What aspects of the event need improvement?
- What did you learn about yourself through this experience?
- What did you learn from others through this experience?

Sustainable Extension

This activity can be implemented in physical education or intramurals as a nontraditional game that can heighten awareness regarding individuals with visual impairments. This game is played in over 100 countries and is one of the most popular Paralympic sports.

Forms and Templates

Sample Time Sheet

SAMPLE TIME SHEET

7:30-9:00	9:00-10:00	10:00-11:00	11:00-12:00	12:00-1:00	1:00-2:00
Setup crew: Set up courts, get out equipment, set up tables Names: —————— —————— ——————	Volunteer staff: Available to answer questions and help (floater) Names: —————— —————— ——————	Volunteer staff: Available to answer questions and help (floater) Names: —————— —————— ——————	Volunteer staff: Available to answer questions and help (floater) Names: —————— —————— ——————	Volunteer staff: Available to answer questions and help (floater) Names: —————— —————— ——————	Cleanup crew: Put away equipment, clean up courts, put away refreshments Names: —————— —————— ——————
	Work registration table Names: —————— —————— ——————	Work registration table Names: —————— —————— ——————	Work registration table Names: —————— —————— ——————	Distribute prizes to championship team Names: —————— —————— ——————	
	Work refreshment stand Names: —————— —————— ——————	Work refreshment stand Names: —————— —————— ——————	Work refreshment stand Names: —————— —————— ——————	Work refreshment stand Names: —————— —————— ——————	

	9:00-10:00	10:00-11:00	11:00-12:00	12:00-1:00	
	Two referees for court 1 Names: —————— —————— ——————	Two referees for court 1 Names: —————— —————— ——————	Two referees for court 1 Names: —————— —————— ——————	Two referees for court 1 Names: —————— —————— ——————	
	Two referees for court 2 Names: —————— —————— ——————	Two referees for court 2 Names: —————— —————— ——————	Two referees for court 2 Names: —————— —————— ——————	Two referees for court 2 Names: —————— —————— ——————	

From J. De Marzo, A. Gibbone, G. Letter, and C. Klein, 2012, *Healthy and sustainable fundraising activities* (Champaign, IL: Human Kinetics).

So You Think You Can Video Dance

Activity Description

This activity raises low to moderate funds while promoting community wellness. Participants of all ages learn the importance of physical activity while benefiting from intergenerational communication and community involvement. A moderate level of knowledge, skills, and abilities is required of both young volunteers and adult leaders. Those involved will compete in a dance-related video gaming tournament to help raise funds through entry fees or sponsorship.

Educational Objectives

Students will:

- Create advertisements on the computer (increasing their technological literacy) or by hand and disseminate information for the event, which will increase their involvement in the organization and in the larger community.
- Value the role dance plays as a lifetime physical activity.
- Create and manage tournament details.
- Assist participants with video gaming equipment.

Adults will:

- Model socially responsible behavior as well as care and concern for neighbors.

The community will:

- Benefit from your organization's interest in promoting socially responsible behavior and community engagement.
- Experience increased cohesiveness from citizens working together.

Targeted Dimensions of Health

Social   **Mental**   **Emotional**   **Spiritual**

Standards Met

National Health Education standards 1, 4, 5, 6, and 7
National Association for Sport and Physical Education standards 1, 2, 5, and 6
21st century student outcomes:

Life and Career Skills   **Learning and Innovation Skills**   **Information, Media, and Technology Skills**

21st century interdisciplinary themes: Financial, economic, business, and entrepreneurial literacy; civic literacy; health literacy; environmental literacy

Age Level

10+

Materials

Music

Speakers and sound system

Electronic dance gaming equipment

Video console (Nintendo, PlayStation, or Xbox) (If you are purchasing equipment, we recommend Nintendo Wii to use at other fundraising and educational events.)

Dance pads

Projector and screen, television, or both

Recommended Procedures

1. Hold an initial committee meeting to recruit volunteers and brainstorm ideas.
2. Provide time for students to practice.
3. Hold an event development meeting.
4. Advertise the event.
5. Conduct the event.
6. Hold a postevent meeting and thank contributors.

Event Preparation Time Line

Eight Weeks Prior to the Event

Meet with your tournament committee, including young volunteers, to choose the date and time as well as the kind of event you want to hold (e.g., for students and faculty only and held during school hours or after school; for students, faculty, and parents and held after school or on a weekend; or for the entire community and held after school or on a weekend).

At this point you will also need to determine the entry fee. If participants will be sponsored, how will that be set up?

Your next task is to decide which game platform(s) to use (e.g., Nintendo, PlayStation, Xbox) and how you will obtain equipment for the event. You can ask participants to bring their own equipment; purchase it from the school, PTA, or organization budget; or rent it. Will you use projectors or televisions, and how many will you need?

Design and distribute marketing materials for recruiting participants. It is important to start recruiting early to give participants time to practice.

Six Weeks Prior to the Event

Six weeks before the event, you should still be recruiting participants. At this time you should also start collecting donations of prizes for winners from local merchants or organizations. To give businesses an incentive for donating, you could have volunteers design a poster or event T-shirt that advertises their sponsorship. Prizes can be awarded for the winner(s) of each game level from beginner to advanced, depending on the game platform.

Five Weeks Prior to the Event

This is the time to hold a planning meeting with volunteers to work out the logistics of the event. Discuss how many participants will compete at the same time, how scores will be recorded, and which scores will be used to determine standings. Who will be supervising the competitions? Will participants play single or multiplayer matches?

This is also the time to decide where the equipment will be stored or delivered and the role of the technology staff or young volunteers in setting up the equipment on the day of the event. Assign volunteers to on-site registration and checking in preregistered participants.

Two to Four Weeks Prior to the Event

As the event gets closer, schedule a series of meetings to keep on top of preparation plans.

One Week Prior to the Event

Plan a meeting a week before the event to confirm volunteers' responsibilities and go over your equipment setup plan. Make sure the members of the registration team are prepared for their responsibilities.

Day of the Event

At the event, take pictures and videos to promote the next event.

After the Event

Send thank-you e-mails or notes to participants and sponsors with a summary of the event outcomes.

Postevent Processing and Evaluation

Discussion Questions for Students

What new skills did you learn in preparing for this event?
What impact has your participation in this event had on you?

Questions for Adults

What experiences were new or different for you during this event?
Are there any modifications to this event that you suggest for similar events in the future?

Sustainable Extension

Dancing is a lifetime activity that can be enjoyed by individuals within a variety of ages and abilities. Dancing is part of social customs and recreation; appreciating music, rhythm creative expression, and physical activity is of value to all. Children and adults alike can engage in dance-related active gaming at home, with friends or relatives, or even in school on a continual basis.

Forms and Templates

Announcement
Participant Registration Form
Merchant and Organization Prize Donation Solicitation Letter
Sponsor Form
Informational Flyer

Do you like to dance or know someone who can dance?

Join us or sponsor someone in a video game dance-off!

Prizes for first, second, and third place at each game level.

Schools have been interested in Dance Dance Revolution (DDR) as a healthy way for children to exercise. DDR is an interactive music video game that provides a healthy, energetic fitness workout performed to high-energy music. Players are challenged to match their dance steps with the flashing arrows on the screen to the beat of chosen music. The game is played by pressing the arrows on the dance pad with your feet in response to the arrows on the screen. The rhythm or difficulty of the arrow patterns depends on your ability to time and position your steps accordingly.

People enjoy video games, and using video game dance programs allows you to be physically active and have fun at the same time. This fundraiser is a fun way to be active with others and raise money for our cause. We are raising money by having people participate in the event on [Date] or by having sponsors support DDR participants.

Contact [Name] at [E-mail address or phone number] for all information, or visit [Website address].

From J. De Marzo, A. Gibbone, G. Letter, and C. Klein, 2012, *Healthy and sustainable fundraising activities* (Champaign, IL: Human Kinetics).

PARTICIPANT REGISTRATION FORM

Name	Contact information	Participation date (if multiple)	Game platform and level	Entry fee (yes/no)	Sponsorship (yes/no)

From J. De Marzo, A. Gibbone, G. Letter, and C. Klein, 2012, *Healthy and sustainable fundraising activities* (Champaign, IL: Human Kinetics).

Dear [Name],

I'm writing on behalf of [Name of organization]. [Letter recipient's name], we need your help with our upcoming event to benefit [Recipient organization]. This event involves [Event description]. I am asking local businesses to show their support by donating prizes to be awarded to first-, second-, and third-place winners. [Thank them for their continued support if they have donated before.] We would appreciate a donation of [Donation item or amount]. Your donation will help us achieve our goal for this fundraiser, which is [Monetary goal]. Your generous donation of [Service or merchandise] will be publicly acknowledged at our event through promotional announcements and flyers, a logo, a prominent note in our program, and [Other benefits they will receive]. We believe that your business will benefit from the community goodwill generated by your kind donation to our group.

Sincerely,

[Name]
Spokesperson
[Phone number]
[E-mail address]

From J. De Marzo, A. Gibbone, G. Letter, and C. Klein, 2012, *Healthy and sustainable fundraising activities* (Champaign, IL: Human Kinetics).

SPONSOR FORM

Name of participant:_____

Name	Contact information	Sponsorship type (how the individual participated)	Amount	Gift	Payment type

Total raised:_____

Please send your sponsorship form and fundraising total to [Name] at [Address].

From J. De Marzo, A. Gibbone, G. Letter, and C. Klein, 2012, *Healthy and sustainable fundraising activities* (Champaign, IL: Human Kinetics).

So You Think You Can Video Dance

[Day], [Date], 7 to 10 p.m.

Do you like to dance or know someone who can dance?

Join us or sponsor someone in a video game dance-off!

Prizes are for first, second, and third place at each game level.

Schools have been interested in Dance Dance Revolution (DDR) as a healthy way for children to exercise. DDR is an interactive music video game that provides a healthy, energetic fitness workout performed to high-energy music. Players are challenged to match their dance steps with the flashing arrows on the screen to the beat of chosen music. The game is played by pressing the arrows on the dance pad with your feet in response to the arrows on the screen. The rhythm or difficulty of the arrow patterns depends on your ability to time and position your steps accordingly.

People enjoy video games, and using video game dance programs allows you to be physically active and have fun at the same time. This fundraiser is a fun way to be active with others and raise money for our cause. We are raising money by having people participate in the event on [Date] or by having sponsors support DDR participants.

Contact [Name] at [E-mail address or phone number] for all information or visit [Website address].

From J. De Marzo, A. Gibbone, G. Letter, and C. Klein, 2012, *Healthy and sustainable fundraising activities* (Champaign, IL: Human Kinetics).

Seniors for Seniors: An Evening of Dance

Activity Description

Seniors for Seniors: An Evening of Dance teaches high school seniors life skills by having them work with community members and help with event planning, design, and management. Volunteers prepare an evening of dance classes for seniors in the community. Dance classes and social dance evenings can be promoted based on the targeted age level and the type of dancing the volunteers have learned and would like to offer. From start to finish, student volunteers are responsible for researching dances, advertising, and teaching classes under supervision. Supervisors should be adults with experience in dance or a willingness to learn about dance to better assist the students. Classes take place over a series of evenings, and various styles of dance are offered. The cost of classes and social dance evenings can be a set price or by donation. Both the dance classes and the social dance evenings can take place in school auditoriums or gymnasiums, or at local dance studios. Local dance studios may offer to donate or reduce the cost of facility use charges if they are able to advertise programs that both the students and older adults can join.

Both participants and student volunteers learn about the various dance styles, and volunteers learn how to teach dance to others, which is a lifetime activity. Money is generated from the cost of the classes, donations, and raffle ticket sales.

Volunteer dance instructors need a series of training and practice sessions prior to the start of the classes. Facility space and music are needed for both dance lessons and socials.

Educational Objectives

Students will:

- Create advertisements on the computer (increasing their technological literacy) or by hand and disseminate information for the event, which will increase their involvement in the organization and in the larger community.
- Value the role dance plays as a lifetime physical activity.
- Create and manage the details of the classes and the social dance evenings.
- Compile music for the event.
- Learn dance techniques and styles and prepare methods of teaching them.

Adults will:

- Model socially responsible behavior as well as care and concern for neighbors.

The community will:

- Benefit from your school's interest in promoting socially responsible behavior and community engagement.
- Experience increased cohesiveness from citizens working together.

Targeted Dimensions of Health

   Social   Mental   Emotional   Spiritual

Standards Met

National Health Education standards 1, 2, 4, 6, and 7
National Association for Sport and Physical Education standards 1, 2, 5, and 6
21st century student outcomes:

| Life and | Learning and | Information, Media, |
| Career Skills | Innovation Skills | and Technology Skills |

21st century interdisciplinary themes: Financial, economic, business, and entrepreneurial literacy; civic literacy; health literacy

Age Level

High school seniors

Materials

Paper for flyers and posters
Access to the Internet
Access to local and community newspapers
Music and a music player
Reception table
Refreshments
Raffle tickets

Recommended Procedures

1. Those with different abilities can participate by playing with the video controller instead of the dance pad.
2. Change the theme of the event by using different active video games.
3. Conduct the event during different times to best meet the needs of the participants (during physical education class time, after school hours, evening hours, or weekends).
4. Purchase electronic equipment if member loans are insufficient.

Event Preparation Time Line

Three Months Prior to the Event

Arrange a meeting with interested volunteers to discuss the event and outline procedures. Both the coordinators and the volunteers can find contact information for senior centers, retirement homes, assisted living homes, YMCAs, and other places frequented by seniors by using Internet search engines and local phone books. They can then use Microsoft Word to create a survey about the types of dance styles and classes seniors prefer. This survey can be delivered by hand or by mail. It may be helpful to offer to present the event and distribute and collect the surveys on site, which can be arranged with the site director.

Sample Survey Questions

What is your favorite style of dance to watch?
What is your favorite style of dance to perform?
What kind of dance have you always wanted to learn?
What days and times of day are you most likely to join a dance class?

Two Months Prior to the Event

Use the results of your survey to determine what dances to teach for the fundraiser and when to schedule classes. Both student volunteers and their supervisors can research dance styles to teach using the school library, public library, and Internet search engines. One useful resource is the book *Teaching Dance to Senior Adults* by Liz Lerman (1984, Charles C. Thomas).

Arrange a time for volunteer dance teachers to practice the dances and practice teaching them to others. Their skill level will determine the types of dances to teach. If you have a budget for outside consultants, find out whether community dance companies or instructors would be willing to coach your volunteer teachers. Offering dance-related businesses free advertising may encourage volunteerism and promote your cause. Practice can take place during physical education classes, lunch, or free periods or after school.

Hold a meeting to determine dance class dates and social dance evening dates. You may decide to hold a series of classes, followed by a social dance evening for different types of dances. The social dance evenings should take place on different dates than the classes; however, having a reception or social dance evening following a dance class is a possible alternative.

At this time, volunteers should create a flyer for the fundraiser using Microsoft Publisher. The flyer should include a description of the dance classes and social dance evenings, dates, time, raffles, donation information, and pictures of people performing the dance styles you will be teaching. Distribute flyers to the centers you have identified in your research by mail or by hand, as well as to students' parents and grandparents.

Allowing participants to register in advance will give you a sense of the number of attendees to expect. Volunteers can be assigned to a site on a given day to collect registration forms, or you can arrange an on-site sign-up session. You can include other fundraising activities as well, such as a raffle or 50-50 drawing, to increase your revenue.

One Month Prior to the Event

Solicit stores and family members to donate prizes for raffles. At this time, volunteer dance teachers are continuing to meet and work on the steps for the classes. Volunteers should also create a playlist for the music for the classes. Others should decide what food and drink items to serve during the social dance evenings. You may want to have volunteers prepare a handout of interesting information, such as the history of the dances they are teaching, to distribute to class participants.

One Week Prior to the Event

At this time, volunteers should make posters showing the raffle prizes and the price of the raffle tickets. Confirm who will do what jobs during the dance classes and the final reception; you will need decorators, a setup crew, money collectors, a music assistant, a water vendor, and someone to gather participants' contact information so you can send acknowledgements and follow-up information later. A person or team should also be prepared to buy or prepare food and drinks for the reception.

Day of the Event

The day of the event, students should arrive early to set up the available equipment. Event workers should accommodate the participants as best as possible from the dance class sessions to the social gatherings. Pictures or videos can be used to use to promote the next event; share the experience with the community through print or online media.

After the Event

Write a thank-you letter to participants and donators that includes how much money the fundraiser raised. Send each participant a letter via regular mail or e-mail.

Postevent Processing and Evaluation

Ask senior teens to reflect on their experience by doing one of the following:

- Write a personal essay regarding how this experience has influenced your life.
- Interview one of the senior citizen participants to gather their view on the experience.

Comments can be shared within an event blog or the school website.

Sustainable Extension

Building relationships between youth and elderly can provide meaningful learning opportunities and personal growth. Through lifetime leisure, recreation, or competitive forms of dancing, individuals can gain skills through physical activity and enjoy the social components associated with lesson interactions and social dance evenings. Community connections with local dance studies can be formed for continued participation.

Beep Baseball

Activity Description

This is a project to raise money through a beep baseball event. In the process, volunteers learn life skills by working with community members and assisting in event planning, design, and management. Although beep baseball is traditionally a sport for the visually impaired, it can be played by all. Sighted participants learn to appreciate how visually impaired athletes participate in sports. This game is fun to play and raises money for a worthwhile cause. Monies are raised through team registration and event raffles.

Beep baseball is an internationally played modified game of baseball in which visually impaired athletes on two teams hit, field, and run to designated bases. All competitors must wear blindfolds. Refer to http://nbba.org/about_game.htm for game specifics.

Your event can include a series of activities for participants and their guests before the main beep baseball tournament or even on a separate day. The scores of all the activities in the series are combined into one score to determine the winners. Following are three activities you could use.

Hitting for Distance

Competitors hit the ball off a tee three times. The best distance of the three determines placement. Measurements are made from the tee to where the ball stops rolling. The distance can be converted to points.

Beep Baseball Stop

Competitors stand on a designated spot. The ball is thrown twice, once to each side or twice to the same side of the competitor. The ball must land within a defined circle to be fair to all competitors. Time is measured from the moment the ball leaves the hand of the thrower until it is secured by the competitor. There is a time limit. Time intervals can be converted to points.

Base Run

Competitors stand at home base and listen for either first or third base to be activated. When the buzzing base is activated, the stopwatch is started and the athlete must run as quickly as possible to the base. The stopwatch is stopped when the athlete touches the base. Bases are approximately five-foot-high (1.5 m) soft foam circular pillars set in a square foam base and are placed 100 feet (30 m) from home base. The running time is converted to points.

Educational Objectives

Students will:

- Create advertisements on the computer (increasing their technological literacy) or by hand and disseminate information for the event, which will increase their involvement in the organization and in the larger community.
- Create and manage tournament details.
- Design event T-shirts.
- Learn the rules and regulations of beep baseball.

Adults will:

- Model socially responsible behavior as well as care and concern for neighbors.

The community will:

- Benefit from your organization's interest in promoting socially responsible behavior and community engagement.
- Experience increased cohesiveness from citizens working together.

Targeted Dimensions of Health

Social   **Mental**   **Emotional**   **Spiritual**

Standards Met

National Health Education standards 1, 2, 4, 6, and 7
National Association for Sport and Physical Education standards 1, 2, 5, and 6
21st century student outcomes:

**Life and
Career Skills**   **Learning and
Innovation Skills**   **Information, Media,
and Technology Skills**

21st century interdisciplinary themes: Financial, economic, business, and entrepreneurial literacy; civic literacy; health literacy

Age Level

10+

Materials

Paper for flyers and posters
Access to the Internet
Access to local and community newspapers
Beep baseball equipment (balls, bases)
Umpire equipment
Score sheets
Posterboard

Recommended Procedures

1. Hold a committee meeting.
2. Gather materials and reserve fields.
3. Publicize the event.
4. Get ready for the event day.

Event Preparation Time Line

Three Months Prior to the Event

Set a date, time, and place (field) for the tournament. Get a committee together to decide when and where to hold the tournament and what the entry fee will be. Create a flyer describing the tournament to send to potential teams. Include the date of the tournament, the type of tournament (such as round robin or double elimination, and whether the activity series will be included), the entry fee, the registration deadline, and a contact person's name and phone number. An entry form should be created to distribute along with the flyer. Set a date by which entries must be submitted so you can draft an appropriate schedule prior to the tournament. Determine the method(s) for distributing the flyer (e.g., postings, e-mail, mailings). Notify local newspapers and post information on your organization's website.

Two Months Prior to the Event

Decide what kind of volunteers you need (e.g., umpires, field judges, base operators, scorekeepers, drivers, food servers, first aid workers, field crew, equipment crew). Choose your head umpires and be sure they know the rules. You will also need a statistician. Set up a schedule to post with the necessary slots for volunteers. Train volunteers on how to perform their tasks, and make sure they know the game rules. As soon as the volunteer schedule is set, notify each volunteer of his or her job and time slot(s). Set up a committee to determine what food to serve at the event. This committee is responsible for planning the refreshment menu, purchasing the food, and serving during the event.

Determine what awards, if any, will be given out at the tournament. Once the awards are determined, they need to be constructed. Young volunteers can design certificates to distribute as awards rather than trophies; T-shirts or other gifts can also be given.

Two Weeks Prior to the Event

Put together a packet of information to mail to the registered teams. Include a copy of the game schedule and any other pertinent information.

Event Day

On the day of the tournament, you need to make sure the bases are set up and plugged in. Someone also needs to be sure that there are plenty of beep baseballs charged and ready to use. Delegate someone to be responsible for balls at the tournament: to distribute them to the fields and to collect them once they are dead. A first aid kit should be available at the field, and you may want to have first aid volunteers (e.g., student nurses, reserve personnel) as well.

The field crew needs to be at the fields a couple of hours prior to the start of the first game to mark the fields (if not already done), set up the bases, and distribute the first batch of balls. Be sure that the fields are marked with field numbers (e.g., Field 1, Field 2). The tournament director should be at the fields to meet with the volunteers and make sure each field is staffed with all of the necessary people. Volunteers should arrive half an hour prior to each game start to get checked in and be ready to start working by the game start time. Ideally, you should have one head umpire, two field judges, one base operator, and one or two scorekeepers at each field. Provide a clipboard with score sheets, pencils and erasers, team roster sheets, and an official set of rules at each field.

Have water and cups at each field. Be sure to assign someone to keep track of the beep baseballs (i.e., collect dead balls and supply new balls). Remind the umpires to try to keep the games on schedule. The tournament director should travel among the fields to be sure things are running smoothly. Assign someone to collect the score sheets and turn them in to the statistician for posting.

After the Event

After the games are over, the field crew needs to pick up all equipment: bases, wires, control boxes, and balls. The statistician should post the stats so the information is available for the awards presentation. As soon as the information is available, hold an awards ceremony. (Be sure the awards are on site for the presentation.) The field crew needs to pick up any remaining equipment following the awards ceremony. Be sure to send thank-you notes to volunteers and donors after the event.

Adapted from the National Beep Baseball Association: www.nbba.org/runningatourney.htm.

Postevent Processing and Evaluation

Those involved can conduct a postevent self-assessment on their contributions using the evaluation rubric (table 4.2).

Table 4.2   Event Planning Rubric

	Contribution description	Comments
Event preparation	Provides suggestions during committee meeting and assumes responsibility before and during the event.	
Event	Contributes effectively and efficiently while performing assigned duties.	
Postevent responsibilities	Provides thoughtful recommendations regarding the outcome of the event and suggestions for improvement. Also completes postevent responsibilities in a timely manner.	

Sustainable Extension

This activity can be used to unite a community as an annual or biannual event. Participants can gain awareness about individuals with visual impairments and how this sport can accommodate a variety of participants. Baseball is an American pastime and many would have an interest in joining this event and enjoying it with their families and friends.

Forms and Templates

Team Registration Form

Team Contact/Billing Form

Team Registration

Due:

Team name:_____

City, state: _____

Year:_____

Team Contacts (please list two):

Name: _____

Address: _____

City, state, zip: _____

Phone number (work): _____

Phone number (home): _____

E-mail address: _____

Name: _____

Address: _____

City, state, zip: _____

Phone number (work): _____

Phone number (home): _____

E-mail address: _____

Team registration fee:_____

Make checks payable to: _____

Send the team registration form along with payment (no later than [Date]) to:

_____

If you have questions concerning this form, please call [Name] at [Phone number].

From J. De Marzo, A. Gibbone, G. Letter, and C. Klein, 2012, *Healthy and sustainable fundraising activities* (Champaign, IL: Human Kinetics).

HIGH-LEVEL FUNDRAISERS

Require experience and strong leadership skills

Chapters 3 and 4 present fundraisers that are easy for teachers, parents, coaches, or administrators to conduct. They are outlined using standard classroom-type lesson plans. This chapter contains fundraising ideas that require a higher level of knowledge, skills, and abilities; organizers of the fundraisers in this chapter need some experience, strong leadership skills, and an ability to multitask. Conducting one or more of the fundraisers in chapters 3 and 4 would be a good warm-up for those presented here.

The process flow chart presented in chapter 1 (see figure 1.1 on pages 5-6) may help with the fundraising activities in this chapter because of their complexity. These activities, although more time consuming than those in previous chapters, have the potential to yield large profits. They are geared toward corporations and social or community commerce (larger organizations or community businesses) and can take place in high-profile locations. Often, one well-crafted high-level fundraiser can take the place of multiple smaller ones throughout the year.

This book is set up so that you can start with an activity in chapter 3 to gain confidence to try more advanced activities in chapters 4 and 5. Your organization may also choose to run several fundraisers concurrently or consecutively over the course of the year.

Keep in mind that the activities throughout this book are presented in a somewhat generic form; our intention is to offer activities that you can adapt to fit your organization's unique mission or agenda. Each of the activities in this chapter use similar forms (advertisement flyer, sample press release, sample newsletter article, sample procurement letter, donation form, and thank-you letter to donor). You'll find samples at the end of the activities, and you can modify them from one activity to another to fit your fundraiser.

Organization Poster

Activity Description

The purpose of this activity is to raise money while recognizing students and local businesses within the community. Posters can be placed throughout the community and at any venue the organization uses (e.g., an ice hockey team poster displayed near the entranceway of the ice rink). This fundraiser benefits businesses by involving them in the community, advertising their services, increasing community patronage of their businesses, and improving their community relations (or image). Students, athletes, or organization members are recognized for their involvement in the organization by having their pictures displayed on posters throughout the community. This is a relatively easy activity to organize, and it can generate substantial funds. It is also sustainable if you include a calendar; each year you can send a new picture of your team or group with the calendar. Renewing the poster each year is also sustainable. See Forms and Templates (page 135 for the poster template).

Educational Objectives

Students will:

- Promote community involvement.
- Learn how businesses get returns on their investments.
- Be introduced to networking.
- Become more aware of services and careers offered in the community.
- Be introduced to the concept of bartering.

Adults will:

- Guide students through the varied roles required to navigate today's living and working environments.
- Help students set goals, work both independently and cooperatively, and use both interpersonal communication skills and problem-solving strategies to work with others toward a common goal.

The community will:

- Benefit from social interactions that promote community involvement and shared responsibility.
- Work alongside and support the activities and efforts of local students and community volunteers.
- Help shape the future of young adult community members.
- Engage students and model prosocial civic behaviors such as accountability and community responsibility.

Targeted Dimensions of Health

Social　　**Mental**　　**Emotional**

Standards Met

National Health Education standards 4 and 8
National Association for Sport and Physical Education standard 6
21st century student outcomes:

**Life and
Career Skills**

**Learning and
Innovation Skills**

**Information, Media,
and Technology Skills**

21st century interdisciplinary themes: Global awareness; financial, economic, business, and entrepreneurial literacy; civic literacy; health literacy; environmental literacy

Age Level

This activity can be spearheaded by one adult and a small group of student volunteers as young as 12 years of age.

Materials

Digital camera
Paper for sponsorship flyers

Recommended Procedures

1. Arrange to have a photo taken.
2. Solicit sponsors and collect their business cards.
3. Create the poster.
4. Distribute posters to sponsors and throughout the community and sell them to members of your organization and their families as well as to local municipalities, the public library, government agencies, and anyplace that sees a lot of community commerce.
5. You can barter ad space for needed services such as the use of a digital camera or photo printer.

Event Preparation Time Line

Week 1: Picture Day

About four weeks from the time you would like the posters posted, schedule a picture day for the members of your organization. They should all wear whatever constitutes your organization's "uniform" (e.g., athletes in full uniform, cast of a play in full costume). At this time you should also create your sponsorship flyer.

Week 2

Once you have had the picture taken for the poster, representatives of your organization should solicit local businesses to become sponsors, using your sponsorship form. Consider bartering with a printing company for a discount on poster printing in exchange for a double ad on the poster. Those who are soliciting should collect a business card from each sponsoring business to use on the poster. Offer each sponsor a free poster and free admission to one of your organization's events (e.g., a free pass to a play performance, free admission to a homecoming game).

Weeks 3 and 4

Once you have all of your sponsors, submit your photo and the sponsors' business cards to the printer to create the poster. Post and distribute the poster throughout the community. Also, make copies of the poster available to other community supporters (e.g., local law enforcement, fire department).

Postevent Processing and Evaluation

Suggested questions include:

- Could this event have been run differently or more efficiently?
- How can you expand your customer base for next year's poster?

Sustainable Extension

In addition to smaller local businesses, you might also consider soliciting the sponsorships of a corporation (e.g., a professional team, a large community employer). If one of your sponsors is a health-oriented food establishment or health club, you could include a healthy recipe or health tip on the poster. Your poster could also double as a schedule announcement by running a schedule along one border of the photo and advertisements along the other three.

One way to save on printing fees is to recruit someone from within your organization to create the poster (e.g., someone from a school art or technology department).

Forms and Templates

Sponsorship flyer
Poster template

[Date]

[Name]
[Address]

Dear [Name],

I would like to invite you to participate in a very special event. For the third year in a row, [Name of organization] will be sponsoring a corporate advertisement poster and calendar to benefit [Recipient organization]. We need local business owners like you to make this year's poster a success.

All proceeds from the advertisement poster will be used to maintain the [List items]. Your donation will allow [Recipient organization] to continue to [Describe work of recipient organization].

The work of the [Recipient organization] is supported by tax deductible contributions made by individuals, companies, and organizations. In return for your financial support of [Amount], we will feature your company business card or logo on a poster alongside a collage of the many people involved in our program. It will also include a yearly calendar of events.

We will display these advertisement posters throughout the community, thus giving your business great exposure. In return for your donation, we will provide you with one free poster and free admission for two at our event.

Thank you in advance for your support of this important event. Together we can support our local community.

Sincerely,

[Name]
Chair

From J. De Marzo, A. Gibbone, G. Letter, and C. Klein, 2012, *Healthy and sustainable fundraising activities* (Champaign, IL: Human Kinetics).

POSTER TEMPLATE

Business card	Business card	Business card	Business card	Business card	Business card
Business card					Business card
Business card	Photo	Photo	Photo	Photo	Business card
Business card	Photo	Photo	Photo	Photo	Business card
Business card	Photo	Photo	Photo	Photo	Business card
Business card	Photo	Photo	Photo	Photo	Business card
Business card	Business card	Business card	Business card	Business card	Business card
Business card					Business card

From J. De Marzo, A. Gibbone, G. Letter, and C. Klein, 2012, *Healthy and sustainable fundraising activities* (Champaign, IL: Human Kinetics).

Corporate–Celebrity Fundraiser

Activity Description

In this high-end fundraising activity, companies pay for the privilege of competing against each other in a sporting event, and the public pays to watch. Ten teams representing 10 companies compete in a sport such as golf, softball, or one of our favorites: dodgeball or kickball. For an added fee, teams may include a celebrity, such as a sport figure, TV or radio personality, newscaster, or local politician. Teams can be made by the company personnel; this establishes a team mentality and gets participants excited to participate.

This event does not require a very high level of knowledge, skills, and abilities, although the organizer must be adept at delineating responsibilities and have a fairly strong network of associates. The greatest challenge is finding event coordinators with connections to celebrities or popular community icons.

Any team wanting to play with a celebrity should be required to pay an additional fee. If there aren't enough celebrities for each team, the highest bidder can win the privilege to play with the celebrity. Consider asking local celebrities to participate on a pro bono basis. They can be team captains or referees if they prefer not to participate athletically. The event committee is responsible for getting celebrities.

The event can be held outside at a local park (weather permitting) or inside at a facility that is rented for the day or a few hours. The size of your venue will determine the size of your event. If it will be held outdoors, always anticipate weather (e.g., rain, wind, snow). Seasonal factors will also affect price and availability. Most often you can arrange either a flat payment for exclusive facility use or a per-game fee. Outdoor community parks are very reasonably priced, and most offer a day use fee with access to facilities.

To maximize attendance, set a reasonable ticket price. Offer attractive special ticket prices such as a flat corporate rate or discounts for corporations that sponsor more than one team. Also, if you are going to have vendors or sponsors at the event, be creative in your pricing structure. You might allow food or beverage vendors to have the opportunity to participate in the event, like a bonus for a reduced fee for their team. You may extend your event by offering a preevent breakfast or a postevent awards meet-and-greet for special guests who want to participate but do not want to engage in the sport.

We suggest soliciting for participants at an office suite that houses several corporations that serve similar clientele (e.g., a pharmaceutical industrial park, an office building that houses several law firms, an industrial park that houses several companies vying for a similar sector of commerce). This takes advantage of the intrinsic competitive nature of corporate culture. Also, it simplifies your advertising and signage efforts and encourages people to talk up the event at the workplace.

Each extension activity (e.g., raffles, photo opportunities for a fee, signed memorabilia, silent auctions) is an opportunity to raise additional funds. In games such as softball and kickball, teams can include 15 people and a celebrity. If each team is paying $1,000, you will make good money in a short afternoon.

Educational Objectives

Students will:

- Work and network with celebrities and companies in the community.
- Observe the willingness of the community to come together for a common cause.
- Help with organizing and scheduling the event.
- Set and achieve personal goals and learn new skills.
- Evaluate the event and their efforts and identify the new skills they gained in the process.

Adults will:

- Mobilize students and community volunteers.
- Use new skills as a result of working on a more challenging fundraising event.
- Demonstrate to students and community volunteers that a coordinated effort can be highly successful and lucrative with the right direction and effort.

The community will:

- Benefit from the social interactions of community adults and student volunteers.
- Support local youth groups.
- Be strengthened by the contributions of local corporations in the form of contacts and skill sets.

Targeted Dimensions of Health

Physical   **Emotional**   **Social**

Standards Met

National Health Education standards 4, 5, 6, and 8
National Association for Sport and Physical Education standards 5 and 6
21st century student outcomes:

Life and   **Learning and**   **Information, Media,**
Career Skills   **Innovation Skills**   **and Technology Skills**

21st century interdisciplinary themes: Global awareness; financial, economic, business, and entrepreneurial literacy; civic literacy; health literacy; environmental literacy

Age Level

Although participants can be of any experience level, we recommend that student participants be high school age or older.

Materials

Scorecards and pencils, which can be donated by local businesses
Sporting equipment (seek the sponsorship of a local sporting goods store or business)
Stereo system or PA setup
Raffle tickets
Flyers
Access to the Internet for e-mail blasts and social networking posts

Recommended Procedures

1. Create an event committee and subcommittees.
2. Designate an event chair to be accountable for the entire event, overseeing all deadlines, materials, and advertising, and ensuring that subcommittees are on task.
3. Arrange for a venue at which to hold the event.
4. Decide whether you want overlapping activities at your event (e.g., Chinese auction, silent auction, raffle, door prizes, photographer to sell photos to participants).
5. Assign a committee to secure celebrities.
6. Get the word out in all forms of media available. Local public access television often provides ad space for free.

Event Preparation Time Line

Week 1

Your first order of business is to set a date for your event and obtain the exclusive use of a field or facility at which to hold it. At this time you should meet with student and adult volunteers and create subcommittees. Suggestions for committees include auction, procurement, arrangements, publicity, setup and cleanup, and banking or cashier.

This is also the time to begin your marketing campaign. This includes posting to your own website; creating flyers; posting to social networking sites; and sending out press releases, invitations to participate, and procurement letters. Procurement letters are for asking corporations or donors for items to be raffled. Consider having a sign-up form on your organization's website, and prepare thank-you letters to send after the event.

Weeks 2 Through 4

This is the time to determine which methods of payment you will accept. The more methods you offer, the easier it is for people to donate. You could arrange to have companies pay online via PayPal. Make sure you have cash on hand to make change on the day of the event. If you will be accepting credit cards, you will need to arrange to have a credit card processing machine.

Volunteers should now be soliciting corporate sponsors. A good place to start is at office parks, where there are many corporations housed in buildings that are set up like a campus. This allows the volunteer to get face time with many potential participants in proximity of one another. Once you secure a few participants from the area, it would be easy to say "Your neighboring office has put two teams in the event; wouldn't you like to represent your company as well?"

Plan how you will set up the event (e.g., a 10-team double-elimination tournament that offers each team two guaranteed games and some teams three or four games depending on how well they play). The Internet has free websites that explain how to arrange matched games (e.g., www.bracketmaker.com, www.printyourbrackets.com/seededbrackets.html, www.teamopolis.com).

Students and adult volunteers should approach local businesses such as restaurants for donations (e.g., food, prizes, giveaways). Some could be invited to participate in alternative ways, such as by providing an on-site barbershop, a photographer, or a DJ. Volunteers can also be distributing flyers or posters throughout the community at this time.

Talk it up, the more noise you make concerning your event, the more people will attend. Send out invitations in as many forms as you can.

If you will be selling raffle tickets, start as soon as possible. Raffle sales can begin before the event; you will be surprised at how many preevent tickets you sell. Consider selling in blocks of 10, 20, or 100 chances. On the day of the event, have adult supervisors or responsible students sell tickets to people as they arrive.

The most attractive raffle prizes are big cash prizes. The second most popular are chances to win smaller cash prizes in addition to the grand prize. You can add smaller noncash prizes that have been donated to increase everyone's chance of winning. Offering prize money of up to 50 percent of the raffle ticket sales can raise a substantial sum. Half of the prize money should be committed to the grand prize, and the balance should be used in declining amounts through at least 10 places (e.g., $500 for first prize, $250 for second prize, $150 for third prize, and so on).

Weeks 5 Through 7

As the event gets closer, you need to designate event day responsibilities to each volunteer. Provide exact locations and detail the responsibilities of and expectations for each volunteer.

Arrange for the final collection of all raffle prizes, door prizes, and awards. Awards should be coupons or gift certificates (e.g., for an all-inclusive trip donated by a local travel agency); no trophies.

Day of the Event

Establish when and where all teams should arrive on the day of the event. Volunteers should be positioned throughout the event area to keep traffic moving. Create multiple signs that list the teams and the tournament schedule, and display them clearly.

Confirm all of the details with the facility. Make sure tables are available, the facility is set up properly, and you have access to electricity and any other services you need. Pick up any items you need to decorate for the event.

After the Event

Once the event has concluded, announce the winners and distribute their awards. Deposit the funds you have collected as soon as possible.

Send thank-you letters to everyone who contributed a prize to the event and to every community sponsor and organization that assisted (see Forms and Templates). Hold a wrap-up meeting with the event committees to discuss what worked well and what should be changed for the next event. Be sure to keep a record of donors for your next event.

Postevent Processing and Evaluation

Discussion Questions for Students

Why is civic engagement important?

Did this activity make you think differently about your community?

How do you think this activity affected the community?

What new skills did you learn from this activity?

Discussion Questions for Adults

What did you learn about mobilizing students and organizing their efforts?

What were some of the pitfalls in organizing community helpers?

Was the community supportive of this event?

How could this event have been more successful?

If you could have done something differently, what would it have been?

Sustainable Extension

Create a pre- or postevent (e.g., a preevent breakfast or postevent cocktail party) where community members can meet and greet celebrities.

Forms and Templates

Team Roster Registration

Informational Flyer

Procurement Letter

Donation Form

TEAM ROSTER REGISTRATION

Please sign up the corporate team _____ [Name of team] for the corporate–celebrity softball tournament to be held [Date] (rain date [Date]) at [Location].

_____ I have enclosed my check or money order for [Amount].

_____ I have enclosed an additional [Amount] for a celebrity player to join our team.

Player 1 name and e-mail address: _____/_____

Player 2 name and e-mail address: _____/_____

Player 3 name and e-mail address: _____/_____

Player 4 name and e-mail address: _____/_____

Player 5 name and e-mail address: _____/_____

Player 6 name and e-mail address: _____/_____

Player 7 name and e-mail address: _____/_____

Player 8 name and e-mail address: _____/_____

Player 9 name and e-mail address: _____/_____

Player 10 name and e-mail address:_____/_____

Player 11 name and e-mail address:_____/_____

Player 12 name and e-mail address:_____/_____

Player 13 name and e-mail address:_____/_____

Player 14 name and e-mail address:_____/_____

Player 15 name and e-mail address:_____/_____

Player 16 name and e-mail address:_____/_____

From J. De Marzo, A. Gibbone, G. Letter, and C. Klein, 2012, *Healthy and sustainable fundraising activities* (Champaign, IL: Human Kinetics).

Corporate–Celebrity Softball Tournament

[Location]

[Address]

[Date]

Please support the [Name of organization]. We are raising funds [Use of funds; e.g., to offset expenses to send our junior development team to the United States Soccer Academy in New York City in the spring].

You can help by participating in our first corporate–celebrity softball tournament. Everyone is welcome to participate. Corporate teams should register together. The fee is [Amount] per team. Several local celebrities have agreed to participate, including [Names of celebrities]. If you would like a celebrity to play on your team, please add [Amount] to your fee.

To register, enter your team's roster on our website at [Website address], where you can pay via PayPal. Feel free to contact [Name] at [Phone number] if you have any questions.

Thank you for supporting the [Recipient organization].

From J. De Marzo, A. Gibbone, G. Letter, and C. Klein, 2012, *Healthy and sustainable fundraising activities* (Champaign, IL: Human Kinetics).

PROCUREMENT LETTER

[Date]

[Name]
[Address]

Dear [Name],

I would like to invite you to participate in a very special event. The [Name of organization] is hosting its first-ever corporate–celebrity softball tournament at [Location] on [Date], and we need your help to make it a success.

All proceeds from the corporate–celebrity softball tournament will be used [Use of funds; e.g., to offset expenses to send our junior development team to the United States Soccer Academy in New York City in the spring].

The work of the [Recipient organization] is supported by tax deductible contributions made by individuals, companies, and organizations like you.

Here's how you can help:

1. Please consider donating a prize item. The item can be donated by you, your employer, or both. Past donations have included [List items; e.g., gift baskets, wine, holiday décor items, food items, electronics]. I have enclosed a donation form for you to complete.

2. Please mark your calendar now and plan to attend the corporate–celebrity softball tournament on [Date]. You will receive more information in the mail. We encourage you to bring a friend and your family for a fun day at the [Location].

Thank you in advance for your support of this important event, [Name]. Together we can make a difference!

Sincerely,

[Name]
Chair

DONATION FORM

[Name of organization]

Thank you for making a contribution to our

Corporate–Celebrity Softball Tournament

Please complete this form and fax it to [Name], event chair, at [Fax number].

Donor name: _____

Organization name: _____

Mailing address: _____

_____

Phone: _____

E-mail: _____

Describe the item you are donating (please be as descriptive as possible):

_____

_____

_____

_____

_____

_____

Approximate retail value: $ _____

Thank you for your support!

From J. De Marzo, A. Gibbone, G. Letter, and C. Klein, 2012, *Healthy and sustainable fundraising activities* (Champaign, IL: Human Kinetics).

Gala

Activity Description

The goal of this fundraiser is to raise substantial funds while creating a social gathering for the community. A gala is a theme-based event that offers entertainment, food, and beverages. For example, your group may want to serve hors d'oeuvres during a silent auction or have a casual buffet with live music and local dance instructors giving lessons.

Because this fundraiser requires strong organizational skills and moderate knowledge, it is best undertaken by high school students or adults. Keep in mind that your gala should appeal specifically to your group. We have held galas in school gymnasiums, public library meeting spaces, universities, and museums. Choose a meeting space that reflects your organization's interest or that of the group you are trying to attract. Spaces that have their own charm, such as museums and libraries, are often available to rent and can be very attractive to supporters. There is a novelty to holding a social event in a space that is typically used differently.

To maximize your profits, price your tickets according to what the experience will offer participants. What does the venue typically charge per person? What foods, entertainment, and special services will you offer? If the venue supports it, you can make your gala a black tie affair; participants will expect to pay more for this type of event. Offer attractive pricing options such as a corporate table rate, four tickets for a flat rate, or discounts for members or families and friends of members.

In addition to ticket sales, your gala can raise funds in a number of creative ways. If you choose to have vendors or specialty services available, those vendors should pay for the opportunity to be present at your event. You might want to include an auction of jewelry, spa services, or other high-end items. Consider offering advertising space on signs at the event or in any of the pre- or postevent literature for businesses that want to contribute but have no interest in attending. Events hosted at museums after hours have fetched thousands of dollars simply by charging extra for the privilege of a private, after-hours viewing of the entire museum collection or particular galleries. Events at wildlife preserves and zoos have done the same (e.g., allowing participants to view new inhabitants or baby animals before they are presented to the public).

Dancing is always an expected activity at a gala. However, these days few people have the opportunity to learn or practice their dance skills. You can offer a dance primer at your event for those who don't know the classic dances. Local dance studio instructors or members of a local college or university dance team might be willing to teach basic steps. This could be an added fee or be included as a free activity.

Consider inviting up-and-coming chefs or established community chefs to serve samples, or "small plates," of their signature dishes at your event. You may ask several local chefs from different food genres to participate, so they are not in direct competition. Or you might invite one chef to serve an appetizer, one to serve a main dish, and one to serve a dessert. Food can be included in the price of admission, or you can charge participants per plate and share the profits as you see appropriate. In this competitive economy, up-and-comers and established restaurateurs are all vying for the same consumers. Many will leap at the opportunity to showcase their talents and be willing to pay you for that opportunity.

Local musicians or choral groups might be willing to pay a small fee to entertain at your event. Professional musicians sometimes contribute by agreeing to perform for a discounted fee. Many college and university groups are glad to perform for the sake of exposure and practice.

At many galas, participants are given goody bags at the end of the evening as a thank-you. Goody bags include things such as samples of perfumes, local delicacies, gift certificates to local businesses, and samples of lotions and beauty products. Many companies are happy to provide freebies or samples if given enough notice and if they believe their efforts will result in future customers. A well-crafted solicitation letter and a good cause are usually all it takes.

Educational Objectives

Students will:

- Be exposed to community spaces that may be unfamiliar to them (e.g., a museum, local college, public library).
- Develop an understanding of marketing and promotion.
- Practice networking and associated social skills.
- Meet business owners and other adults within the community.

Adults will:

- Be exposed to community spaces that may be unfamiliar to them (e.g., a museum, local college, public library).
- Teach students marketing, promotion, and networking strategies that can serve them in the future.
- Practice their own networking skills.
- Establish new networking contacts and professional and social relationships with other community members.

The community will:

- Benefit from their involvement because the experience is likely to provide an opportunity for prosocial involvement; all participants will benefit from the civic engagement.
- Have exposure to community spaces that may be new to them (e.g., museum, local college, public library).
- Assist student volunteers in developing and understanding marketing, promotion, and networking principles that can serve them in the future.
- Practice their own networking skills.
- Foster new networking contacts and professional or social relationships with the student community and their families and other adult supporters.

Targeted Dimensions of Health

Social

Mental

Emotional

Standards Met

National Health Education standards 4, 5, 6, and 8
National Association for Sport and Physical Education standards 2, 5, and 6
21st century student outcomes:

**Life and
Career Skills**

**Learning and
Innovation Skills**

**Information, Media,
and Technology Skills**

21st century interdisciplinary themes: Global awareness; financial, economic, business, and entrepreneurial literacy; civic literacy; health literacy; environmental literacy

Age Level

This activity requires a few adults to oversee student volunteers who could be as young as 12 years old.

Materials

Paper for flyers
Access to the Internet (for website announcements, an e-mail blast, and social networking posts)

Recommended Procedures

1. Designate an event chair and create an event committee.
2. Create subcommittees for each area of the event. Have certain groups secure the venue, take charge of entertainment, lead the advertising in print media, lead development of online media blasts, and so on.
3. After choosing a venue, consider the size of the event you want to hold, your organization's financial resources, and the interests of potential attendees.
4. Secure participating chefs or restaurants; choose what dishes will be served. If you will have more than one chef or restaurant, think about the dishes being served and make sure they don't compete with one another.
5. You will need a committee to handle all monies and might have a several ways in which people can pay for the event and the food provided at the event.

Event Preparation Time Line

Weeks 1 and 2

After setting the date and time of your event, secure the venue and establish the theme. If you plan to have your event outdoors, be sure to anticipate inclement weather (e.g., rain, wind, snow). Most often you will pay a flat fee for the exclusive use of an entire facility or a space within a multiuse facility. Be sure to consider the resources of your organization and the desires of your potential audience.

You will need an experienced event chair to oversee your subcommittees, materials, and advertising, and to keep a close eye on deadlines. At this time you should also create subcommittees to take care of the nuts and bolts of the event.

Now is also the time to book the entertainment and caterers for your event. See the preceding Activity Description for some suggestions, but always consider the unique interests of your targeted population. You can be creative here. Once you have your gala mapped out, send "save the date" cards to the community. These can be sent out to individuals, family members of participants and volunteers, community organizations, the fire department, school districts, and local hospitals. Remember to get the most out of your advertising efforts. Your group can brainstorm potential participant markets.

Weeks 3 Through 5

Now that you have an outline of your gala and have alerted the community that it's happening, it's time to personally invite local vendors and businesses to participate. Consider offering a pair of gala tickets in exchange for a donated prize that could be used in a raffle or as an item for the silent auction. Send out donor solicitation letters to companies for samples or freebies to put in your goody bags.

Publicize your event through every medium possible, depending on your financial resources. If you can, advertise in local newspapers and on local radio stations (some offer free public service announcements). If you have an e-mail list, send regular announcements about your gala. Don't forget social networking sites—which are a popular way people connect these days.

Make tickets easy to purchase by setting up an online purchasing option. PayPal is the most commonly used online payment company and is easy to use. If you are not familiar with it, now is the time to learn. Electronic invitations and announcements can contain e-links to your payment site to make it really easy for people to buy tickets.

Weeks 6 Through 8

Gather the materials you need to decorate the venue according to your established theme. Solicit food and beverage providers for donations. This is also a time to contact special guests or celebrities if you are planning to offer special seating sections, private viewings, or a chance to meet important people.

Even small events need some type of security and attention to parking. Confirm these arrangements at this time.

Weeks 9 Through 11

As your gala date approaches, both student and adult volunteers should be trained in their duties. Be sure they know exactly how you want them to perform their assigned tasks. Responsible students can act as docents for museum exhibits or particular installations.

Firm up your itinerary (i.e., schedule of events) and send it in a final e-mail to everyone involved. You will certainly want to send an itinerary to all organizers so they know what is expected of them and where they are needed. You could also e-mail the evening's events or send an e-mail blast to committed participants. Collect all door prizes and raffle prizes, and proofread any signs you plan to post before printing them.

Week 12

Just before the gala, hold a meeting of all volunteers and committee chairs to discuss any unresolved issue and last-minute details. Make sure all volunteers know their duties and the times they need to arrive at the venue. Committee chairs should confirm the attendance of all invited celebrities and VIPs, sponsors, chefs, entertainers, and vendors.

Day of the Event

The most important things on the day of the event are to arrive early, expect the unexpected, be flexible, and enjoy your night. Set up a sign-in book to gather names, e-mail addresses, street addresses, and other contact information from attendees so you can create a mailing list for next year's event and send out thank-yous.

After the Event

As soon after the gala as possible, deposit the funds. Send thank-you letters to everyone who contributed: community sponsors and any organizations that provided assistance. Also send attendees thank-you letters; this can be done very easily electronically and then names can be saved for next year's event. Organizers can build a database of individuals. Submit a press release to local papers sharing your success and thanking the community for its support. Hold a wrap-up meeting with all the subcommittees to discuss what worked well and what could be changed for the next event.

Postevent Processing and Evaluation

Discussion Questions for Students

Why is civic engagement important?
Did this event make you think differently about your community?
How did this event affect the community?
What new skills did you learn from this event?

Discussion Questions for Adults

What did you learn about mobilizing students and organizing their efforts?
What were some of the pitfalls in organizing community helpers?
Was the community supportive of this event?
How could this event have been more successful?
If you could have done something differently, what would it have been?

Sustainable Extension

For this event you might want to invite local celebrities; everyone wants to rub elbows with the rich and famous. You might provide photo opportunities with the celebrities for a fee. Additionally, as mentioned in the introduction, many people are not skilled in formal dance styles. You might have the local college dance team or professional instructors coach people in one of the classic dances for a fee. This is a take on the dollar dance held at many weddings, where guests pay a dollar to dance with the bride or groom so that the couple will have extra cash.

Forms and Templates

Advertisement Flyer
Sample Press Release
Sample Newsletter Article

You are invited to the Annual Charity Gala: [Name of event]

Dinner, Silent Auction, Dancing, and Entertainment

[Date]

[Time]

[Location]

Sponsorship Information

Gala sponsor—[Amount]—Two tables (20 seats) and sponsor benefits
Hospitality sponsor—[Amount]—One table (10 seats) and sponsor benefits
Table host—[Amount]—One table (10 seats)

Registration

Couple registration—[Amount]—Two registrations
Individual registration—[Amount]—One registration

Order of Events (Tentative)

[List times and events]
You may purchase tickets at our website: [Website address]

From J. De Marzo, A. Gibbone, G. Letter, and C. Klein, 2012, *Healthy and sustainable fundraising activities* (Champaign, IL: Human Kinetics).

For Immediate Release

CONTACT: [Name] at [Phone number]

Annual Charity Gala: [Name of event]

[Town/city and state]—[Name of organization] will hold its annual charity gala on [Date] at [Location]. All proceeds will go to [Recipient organization] to [Describe work of recipient organization].

[Recipient organization] is currently soliciting donations for this gala event. Last year's event raised over [Amount]. If you would like to contribute supplies, make a monetary donation, or attend the event, please contact [Name] at [Phone number] or check out our website at [Website address].

From J. De Marzo, A. Gibbone, G. Letter, and C. Klein, 2012, *Healthy and sustainable fundraising activities* (Champaign, IL: Human Kinetics).

[Town/city and state]—This past weekend the [Name of organization] held its annual charity gala at [Location]. In attendance were [Names of important people in attendance]. The event raised over [Amount] for [Recipient organization]. [Recipient organization] would like to thank all those in attendance and all the supporters who made this event a huge success. Special thanks to [Names and organizations].

From J. De Marzo, A. Gibbone, G. Letter, and C. Klein, 2012, *Healthy and sustainable fundraising activities* (Champaign, IL: Human Kinetics).

Mini Golf Tournament

Activity Description

This is a community and family-focused event involving 18 or 36 foursomes that compete in a mini golf tournament with a scramble format. Teams start at a particular hole and cycle through all holes. Teams do not have to start at the first hole; you want as many participants playing and cycling through the course as possible. Each foursome pays a buy-in fee, and all participants have opportunities to purchase mulligans and raffle tickets, participate in a silent auction, and win prizes (e.g., for a hole-in-one). Barbecue-style food is offered "at the turn," which is the golfer's intermission (seek donations from local restaurants). One of the biggest challenges with this event is conducting several smaller activities to run concurrently with the golf tournament.

To maximize attendance, price your tickets reasonably. The foursome fee will depend on your target audience. Professionals will likely pay more to sponsor corporate teams than a family would. Corporate entities will often pay to enter five teams of four; you can charge them a higher fee. Consider offering attractive pricing options such as a flat rate for a team or family ticket and discounts for vendors, students, or sponsors. You may want to extend this event by offering a pretournament breakfast or a posttournament meet-and-greet for those who want to participate but do not want to golf.

A great way to raise extra money is to charge foursomes for mulligans (i.e., do-overs) before the event (e.g., three for a set price). These add a lot of fun to the tournament and can generate a handsome return.

Some organizations offer a prize to the first golfer to get a hole-in-one. Such prizes can range from cash to more extravagant items. Some events have offered a new car as the hole-in-one prize. You can take out insurance to cover the cost of the prize in the unlikely event that a hole-in-one occurs. All participants who want to participate in the hole-in-one competition pay an extra fee, which is considerable (to offset the cost of the insurance).

Arrange for each hole to be sponsored by a local business or organization, and post a sign at each hole announcing the sponsor. Sponsors who would like to make their holes more exciting might offer an additional prize (e.g., for hitting into a rain gutter or under a ladder and then into the hole). You can also decorate the holes according to themes that reflect the sponsoring businesses (e.g., hardware, florist, toy store). Of course, businesses pay for sponsoring holes along the course.

Hole sponsors should also be listed in the tournament program, which is another opportunity to raise funds for the event. Businesses that are not interested in participating in the tournament itself could be invited to advertise in the program.

Another option for increasing the visibility and excitement of your event is to invite celebrities to join. Participants wanting to play with a celebrity pay an additional fee. Consider inviting sport figures, TV or radio personalities, newscasters, or local politicians. You might also want to add to the festive atmosphere by having volunteers dress as cartoon characters and offer players the opportunity to golf with their favorite action heroes or characters.

Educational Objectives

Students will:

- Interact with members of the community.
- Demonstrate responsible behavior at a community-based event.
- Participate in a fun event to raise money for a good cause.
- Witness the willingness of the community to come together for a common cause.
- Learn about fair play, teamwork, and leadership.

Adults will:

- Organize several activities simultaneously.
- Oversee student volunteers and community helpers and ensure that they follow through with their assigned tasks and obligations.
- Model leadership skills and demonstrate socially responsible behavior.

The community will:

- Support the efforts of the school or organization.
- Benefit from an increased awareness of organizations that are promoting healthy and socially responsible activities for the community.

Targeted Dimensions of Health

Physical   **Social**   **Mental**   **Emotional**

Standards Met

National Health Education standards 4, 5, and 6
National Association for Sport and Physical Education standards 2, 5, and 6
21st century student outcomes:

Life and
 Career Skills   **Learning and**
 Innovation Skills   **Information, Media,**
 and Technology Skills

21st century interdisciplinary themes: Global awareness; financial, economic, business, and entrepreneurial literacy; civic literacy; health literacy; environmental literacy

Age Level

Participants can range from children to adults and can be of varied experience levels. Consider designating specific tee times for like-aged participants (e.g., morning for students, afternoon for young adults, and evening for adults and professionals).

Materials

Scorecards and pencils (seek donations from a local printer or business)
Golf balls (optional; seek donations from a local sporting goods store or business)
Stereo system or PA
Raffle tickets
Flyers
Access to the Internet (for website and social networking posts and e-mail blasts)

Recommended Procedures

1. Create an event committee and designate an event chair to oversee the work of all subcommittees.
2. Create subcommittees.
3. Set the date for your tournament and choose a venue.
4. Decide what overlapping activities you want at this event, such as the following: Chinese auction, silent auction (items can be placed alongside holes to keep each hole interesting), raffle, door prizes, food and beverage sales (e.g., "barbecue at the turn"), scrip sales, cell phone recycling drop-off zone, video dance competition, and local photographer to take photos to sell to participants.
5. Solicit sponsors and donors.
6. Finalize details for the day of the event.

Event Preparation Time Line

Week 1

Set a date for your event and obtain the exclusive use of a miniature golf facility or convention space (if you are conducting an indoor event). Meet with your student and adult volunteers and create subcommittees (e.g., auction, procurement, arrangements, publicity, physical setup and cleanup, banking or cashier).

Marketing is crucial for ensuring the success of your event. You should begin by publicizing it on your organization's website and providing an online sign-up form there. Create flyers to distribute throughout the community, and post on social networking sites. Ask members of your organization to keep the buzz going by reposting your posts. Send press releases to local media outlets and procurement letters to potential donors and sponsors. At this point you should also have thank-you letters drafted and ready to send after the event.

Weeks 2 Through 4

Determine which methods of payment you will accept. The more methods you offer, the easier it is for people to buy. Make sure you have cash on hand to make change on the day of the event. Arrange for a credit card processing machine if you will be accepting credit cards. Participants will be urged to pay ahead of time; this way you know how many people you can expect. Organizers sometimes let registrants pay as they arrive.

Now is the time to solicit sponsors and donors. Send students and adult volunteers to local businesses and restaurants to request donations of food, prizes, and giveaways. Invite local businesses to sponsor a hole or participate in alternative ways (e.g., barbershop on site, photographer, DJ).

Talk up your event. The more noise you make, the more people will attend. Send out invitations to community members in as many forms as you can.

If you will be selling raffle tickets, decide how you will sell them. Raffle sales can begin prior to the event; you will be surprised at how many presales you will have. Consider selling tickets in blocks of 10, 20, or 100. You can also have adult supervisors or responsible students sell tickets to people as they arrive for the tournament.

The most attractive raffle prizes are big cash prizes. The second most popular are smaller cash prizes. You can add smaller noncash prizes that have been donated, so that everyone entered has a better chance of winning something. You can offer prize money of up to 50 percent of raffle ticket sales and still raise a substantial sum. Half of the prize money should be committed to the grand prize, and the balance should be used in declining amounts through at least 10 places (e.g., $500 for first prize, $250 for second prize, $150 for third prize, and so on).

Weeks 5 Through 7

At this point all volunteers should be very clear about their event-day responsibilities. Arrange for the final collection of all raffle prizes, door prizes, and awards. Awards should be coupons or gift certificates (e.g., for an all-inclusive trip donated by a local travel agency); no trophies.

Establish tee times for all participants. You will want volunteers along the course to keep traffic moving. Create multiple signs that show teams and tee times, and display them clearly.

Confirm all the details with the facility (e.g., tables are set up and you have access to electricity and any other services you might need). Pick up any items you will need to decorate for the event.

Day of the Event

Mini Golf Tournament

Arrive early! Set up signs, the awards table, tables for refreshments (if applicable), and a cashier's table. During the event, be mindful of time constraints; announce periodically how much time is left for raffle ticket purchases and before the start of tee times. Encourage participants to donate in other ways (e.g., monetary donations). Have a participant registry so that you can get e-mail or street addresses from all attendees to send out thank-you notes and announcements of next year's event.

Auction

After the auction closes, gather up all bid sheets and tally the results. You may hold a raffle for another item or have people from your organization speak or entertain the participants during the tallying. (Establish a method for tallying bids before the event with your banking team.) Once the event has concluded, announce the winners and distribute prizes.

After the Event

Deposit the funds as soon as possible after the event. Send thank-you letters or e-mails to all prize donors and to all sponsors and organizations that assisted with the event (see Forms and Templates). Hold a wrap-up meeting with the subcommittees to discuss what worked well and what could be changed for your next event. Keep a record of donors for your next event.

Postevent Processing and Evaluation

Discussion Questions for Students

Why is civic engagement important?

Did this event make you think differently about your community?

How did this event affect your community?

What new skills did you learn from this event?

Discussion Questions for Adults

What did you learn about mobilizing students and organizing their efforts?

What were some of the pitfalls in organizing community helpers?

Was the community supportive of this event?

How could this event have been more successful?

If you could have done something differently, what would it have been?

Sustainable Extension

Include celebrities in each foursome or at specific holes (e.g., "beat the pro" competition). Conduct the event indoors at a convention facility. Each room could have a hole for each sponsor. A conference center, banquet facility, convention center, or some large hotels often have several rooms that can be separated by walls or the walls can be removed for an open space. Also create a pre- or postevent (e.g., a pretournament breakfast or post-tournament cocktail party where people can meet and greet pros or local celebrities) for those who may want to participate or contribute but are not interested in mini golf.

Forms and Templates

Informational Flyer

Mini Golf Tournament

to benefit

[Name of organization]

[Address]

Please help us raise funds [Use of funds; e.g., to offset expenses to send our junior development team to the United States Soccer Academy in New York City in the spring].

We are hosting our first mini golf tournament at [Location] on [Date]. Everyone is welcome to participate. Foursomes should register together. The fee is [Amount] per foursome. Several local celebrities have agreed to participate in this event, including [Names of celebrities]. If you would like to invite one of these celebrities to be a part of your foursome, please add [Amount] to your registration fee (foursomes with a celebrity pay [Amount]).

Thank you for supporting [Recipient organization].

Please sign up the following foursome for the mini golf tournament on [Date], at [Location].

_____ We have enclosed a check or money order for [Amount] for our foursome.

_____ We have enclosed an additional [Amount] for a celebrity player to join our foursome.

Player 1 name and e-mail address: _____ / _____

Player 2 name and e-mail address: _____ / _____

Player 3 name and e-mail address: _____ / _____

Player 4 name and e-mail address: _____ / _____

From J. De Marzo, A. Gibbone, G. Letter, and C. Klein, 2012, *Healthy and sustainable fundraising activities* (Champaign, IL: Human Kinetics).

Friday Night at the Museum With Chefs' Dinner

Activity Description

This activity raises substantial funds while providing a social gathering for the community. It includes entertainment and the sale of chef-prepared gourmet food and beverages in the unique environment of a museum. Adult organizers and their student volunteers need strong organizational skills and moderate knowledge to create a successful event. This event is particularly special because the venue lends a novel twist to your fundraiser.

Throughout the United States, museums are increasingly expanding their community involvement by offering live music, exciting and out-of-the-box discussion groups, and behind-the-scenes curatorial tours led by local academicians and knowledgeable laypeople. Dynamic presentations, extended hours, and innovative programming draw audiences to these very special community venues.

Museums generally attract an upscale crowd, including corporate businesspeople who prefer the quiet classiness of a museum to the local bar scene they sometimes frequent with prospective clients. Museum spaces have built-in charm, and people are drawn to the novelty of attending a social event at a space that is typically used differently.

This fundraiser is best conducted alone, without other smaller fundraising activities such as silent auctions, door prizes, or raffles. Such supplemental activities tend to reduce the impact of the larger event.

Museums almost always offer a flat rental fee and exclusive use of the facility. If you decide to hold your museum night on an outdoor patio or terrace, be prepared for weather such as rain and strong winds.

Before engaging chefs, be sure to research them. If your organization is trying to raise funds for the Ocean Preservation Society, you would not want to hire a chef who serves seafood that comes from animals on the endangered species list. Before hiring musicians, consider the nature of their music and the acoustics of the space. The Great Hall in the Museum of Natural History in New York City is awesome, but it might be overwhelming for a jazz group with improper equipment.

To maximize your profits, price your tickets according to the experience you are providing. What does the museum typically charge per person for events such as yours? What does your local celebrity chef generally charge? If appetizers at the chef's restaurant cost $9.00, charge less for the "small plate" you will be offering your supporters (i.e., a half serving of the dish). Small plates allow participants to try more than one of the offerings. When pricing tickets, also keep in mind that you will be selling gourmet dishes and adult drinks (can be nonalcoholic) a la carte.

Offer attractive ticket pricing options such as a corporate table rate, four tickets for a flat rate, or museum member discounts. If you make your event a black tie affair, participants will expect to pay more. You can also offer local businesses space on signage at the event or in any of the pre- or postevent literature. This raises additional funds while not muddying the event with additional vendors.

Some events have raised thousands of dollars simply by offering after-hours, private viewings of the entire museum collection or particular galleries for an additional fee. Local academics or university researchers might be willing to lead a brief discussion about the museum's galleried exhibit following or during the viewing.

You can ask several local chefs from different food genres to participate, so they are not in direct competition. Or you might invite one to offer an appetizer, one to offer a main dish, and one to offer a dessert. In this competitive economy, new and established restaurateurs are vying for the same consumers. Many will leap at the opportunity to showcase their talents and be willing to pay you for that opportunity.

Local musicians or choral groups might be willing to pay a small fee to entertain at your event. Professional musicians sometimes contribute by agreeing to perform for a discounted fee. Many college and university groups are glad to perform for the sake of exposure and practice.

Educational Objectives

Students will:

- Be exposed to a community space that may be unfamiliar to them.
- Learn about marketing and promoting events.
- Learn and practice social and interpersonal networking skills.
- Meet business owners and other adults from the community.

Adults will:

- Be exposed to a community space that may be unfamiliar to them.
- Teach student volunteers marketing, promotion, and networking strategies that can serve them in the future.
- Practice their own networking skills.
- Develop new professional and social relationships and contacts with other community members.

The community will:

- Benefit when seeing that your organization is more than self-serving. Community members will also be part of the process of promoting socially responsible behavior and civic engagement.
- Have exposure to community spaces that may be new to them.
- Assist student volunteers in developing and understanding marketing, promotion, and networking principles that can serve them in the future.
- Practice their own networking skills.
- Foster new networking contacts and professional or social relationships with the student community and their families and other adult supporters.

Targeted Dimensions of Health

Social

Mental

Emotional

Standards Met

National Health Education standards 4, 5, 6, and 8
National Association for Sport and Physical Education standards 2, 5, and 6
21st century student outcomes:

**Life and
Career Skills**

**Learning and
Innovation Skills**

**Information, Media,
and Technology Skills**

21st century interdisciplinary themes: Global awareness; financial, economic, business, and entrepreneurial literacy; civic literacy; health literacy; environmental literacy

Age Level

This activity requires a few adults to organize and head committees and oversee student volunteers. We recommend high-school-aged students.

Materials

Paper for flyers and hard-copy press releases
Access to the Internet for website announcements, e-mail blasts, and social networking posts

Recommended Procedures

1. Create an event committee and subcommittees.
2. Designate an event chair to be accountable and oversee all deadlines, materials, and advertising, and to oversee all subcommittees.
3. Arrange for a venue at which to hold your event.
4. Set the date for your event.
5. Decide what overlapping activities you want at this event, such as the following: Chinese auction, silent auction, raffle, door prizes, food and beverage sales, scrip sales, cell phone recycling drop-off zone, and local photographer to take photos to sell to participants.

Event Preparation Time Line

Weeks 1 and 2

Set a date and time for your museum night event, and arrange for the use of the museum. Set up an event committee and designate a chair before creating subcommittees to take care of the many details. An important role to fill is that of the banker, or cashier. This person is responsible for adding up each purchaser's food and drink purchases and collecting money. The banker also determines which methods of payment will be accepted (credit cards, checks) and makes sure to have cash on hand for change. If you decide to accept credit cards, you will need to arrange some method for processing these payments.

Now is the time to choose and invite chefs and book any entertainment you will be offering. To give people ample time to plan, and to generate excitement for your event, send "save the date" cards to the community. You could also use social media networks and e-mail blasts for announcements.

Weeks 3 Through 5

Personally invite local vendors and businesses to attend. You might offer them a pair of tickets in exchange for an in-kind donation. Publicize your event through any and every medium possible at this point. Make tickets easy to purchase by providing online purchasing options such as PayPal, and e-links to payment sites from your e-mail invitations.

Weeks 6 Through 8

If you are decorating the museum space in any way, this is the time to gather any materials you will need. Contact beverage and food sponsors to confirm with vendors who have already promised donated items or services. If you are offering special VIP privileges such as seating in a special section, a private viewing of the museum collection, or exposure to celebrities, contact anyone you think might be interested. Finally, make arrangements for any security and parking needs you might have.

Weeks 9 Through 11

All students and adult volunteers need specific training in what to do and how to do it. Now is the time to provide that training. Consider offering responsible students the opportunity to act as docents for museum exhibits or particular installations.

Firm up your itinerary (i.e., schedule of events) and send it in a final e-mail to every organizer and vendor involved. Ensure that signs have been proofread for any spelling or grammatical errors before printing them.

Week 12

A week or so before your event, hold a meeting of all volunteers and committee chairs to discuss any unresolved issues and last-minute details. Assign all volunteers their duties, and let them know what time they are expected to arrive at the event. All committee chairs should confirm the attendance of all invited participants, sponsors, chefs, entertainers, and service providers.

Day of the Event

The most important things on the day of the event are to arrive early, expect the unexpected, be flexible, and enjoy your night. Set up a sign-in book to gather names, e-mail addresses, street addresses, and other contact information from attendees so you can create a mailing list for next year's event and send out thank-you letters.

After the Event

As soon after the event as possible, deposit the funds. Send thank-you letters to everyone who contributed: community sponsors and any organizations that provided assistance. Also send attendees thank-you letters; this can be done very easily electronically and then names can be saved for next year's event. Submit a press release to local papers sharing your success and thanking the community for its support. Hold a wrap-up meeting with all the subcommittees to discuss what worked well and what could be changed for the next event.

Postevent Processing and Evaluation

Discussion Questions for Students

Why is civic engagement important?
Did this activity make you think differently about your community?
How do you think this activity affected the community?
What new skills did you learn from this activity?

Discussion Questions for Adults

What did you learn about mobilizing students and organizing their efforts?
What were some of the pitfalls in organizing community helpers?
Was the community supportive of this event?
How could this event have been more successful?
If you could have done something differently, what would it have been?

Sustainable Extension

If there is a new installation at the museum, you might charge a small extra fee for a private viewing of the exhibit. Perhaps you can get the museum to donate a yearlong membership to the museum and then sell raffle tickets for an additional fee. And you might commission young artists to display their works for a fee and allow participants to purchase these items on the eve of the gala.

Forms and Templates

Thank-You Letter to Donor

THANK-YOU LETTER TO DONOR

[Date]

[Name]
[Address]

Dear [Name],

Thank you for your generous tax deductible donation to our Friday night at the museum with chefs' dinner event.

Thanks to you and donors like you, we raised [Amount], which is more than what we raised last year. These funds will continue to support [Work of recipient organization].

We are planning to hold this event again next year and will try to increase the number of donated items and money raised for [Recipient organization]. We hope we can count on your support then.

Thank you again for your generosity.

Sincerely,

[Name]
Chair

From J. De Marzo, A. Gibbone, G. Letter, and C. Klein, 2012, *Healthy and sustainable fundraising activities* (Champaign, IL: Human Kinetics).

Bibliography

Center for Science in the Public Interest. (2007, February 14). Sweet deals: School fundraising can be healthy and profitable, says CSPI. Retrieved October 24, 2011, from www.cspinet.org/new/200702141.html.

Feingold, R. (1999). *Position on adult roles*. Little Falls, NY: NYS AHPERD.

Fernandez, D. (1999). Grant writing tips. Retrieved January 4, 2011, from www.k12grants.org/tips.htm.

Gordon, P., Hilton, R., & Welsch, G. (1988). *Budgeting: Profit planning and control*. Upper Saddle River, NJ: Prentice Hall.

Johnson, L., & Lamb, A. (2007). Grants and grant writing. Retrieved January 4, 2011, from www.eduscapes.com/tap/topic94.htm.

The Joint Commission on National Health Education Standards, American Cancer Society. (2007). *National health education standards: Achieving excellence* (2nd ed.). Atlanta, GA: American Cancer Society.

Kirkwood, J. (2010). Using the social web to drive real-world social action. Retrieved July 7, 2011, from http://handsonblog.org/tag/crowdrise/.

Lerman, L. (1984). *Teaching dance to senior adults*. Springfield, IL: Charles C. Thomas.

Levine, A. (2001). Production budget. Retrieved January 13, 2012, from www.mcli.dist.maricopa.edu/authoring/studio/guidebook/budget_pre.html.

Robbins, S.P. (1997). *Essentials of organizational behavior*. Upper Saddle River, NJ: Prentice Hall.

Vohwinkle, J. (n.d.). How to create a budget. Retrieved October 25, 2011, from http://financialplan.about.com/od/budgetingyourmoney/ht/createbudget.htm.

About the Authors

Jenine M. De Marzo, EdD, is an assistant professor of health education in the department of health studies, physical education, exercise science, and sport management at Adelphi University in Garden City, New York.

De Marzo has more than 20 years of experience teaching health and physical education in public and private school settings with diverse populations. She also has experience in several areas of community and public health as well as over 20 years of experience as a professional and volunteer coach working with youth and young adults in college and community programs.

She is past president of the Higher Education Section for the New York State Alliance for Health, Physical Education, Recreation and Dance (NYS AHPERD). She is also a member of the Teaching Personal and Social Responsibility (TPSR) International Alliance.

De Marzo, her husband, Christopher, and their three children, Arianna, Vittorio, and Giovanni, live in Rockville Centre, New York. In her free time she enjoys running, camping, and playing softball and soccer.

Anne Gibbone, EdD, is an assistant professor in the department of health studies, physical education, exercise science, and sport management at Adelphi University in Garden City, New York. She teaches in the physical education teacher preparation program, specializing in pedagogy and technology integration.

Gibbone earned her doctorate from Teachers College, Columbia University. She is a certified adapted physical educator (CAPE). Formerly, she worked as a physical education teacher and youth athletics coach in a variety of settings and sports, including volleyball, basketball, and lacrosse. She also played and coached both volleyball and lacrosse at the collegiate level. Gibbone has been an executive board member of the New York State Alliance for Health, Physical Education, Recreation and Dance (NYS AHPERD) since 2008.

Greg Letter, PhD, is currently an associate professor and program director of the undergraduate and graduate sport management programs at Adelphi University. Prior to his seven years at Adelphi University, he was an assistant professor and program director of the undergraduate sport communication and graduate sport administration programs at Mississippi State University for three years and an assistant professor and program director of the undergraduate sport management and sport management MBA program at Webber International University for one year. Major responsibilities included teaching, curriculum review and development, marketing programs, internship placement, community outreach and service, and alumni tracking and relations.

Greg earned his PhD in administration and teaching with a concentration in sport administration from the University of Southern Mississippi (USM) in 2001. Before becoming a professor, he spent roughly four years as a graduate assistant under the vice president of administrative affairs and two years as a graduate teaching assistant in the sport administration program at USM. He also has retail management experience at Jumbo Sports, several years of marketing and management experience, minority ownership of Independence Brewing Company (Philadelphia), and roughly five years of teaching and coaching experience in Philadelphia School District, Montgomery County School District (Pennsylvania), and St. Aloysius Academy in Bryn Mawr, Pennsylvania.

Dr. Catherine Klein, PhD, is an online educator in athletic administration for Northcentral University. Klein played for the Canadian national team from 1987 to 1990 and graduated from the State University of New York at Cortland in 1987 with a bachelor's degree in physical education. She earned her master's degree from Kent State University in 1991 and a PhD in sport administration from the University of New Mexico in 2007. She has coached youth, high school, college, and university soccer teams all over the United States. Klein now resides permanently in Ontario, Canada, where she is actively involved in youth sport settings.